GOD WILL GET YOU THROUGH THIS

HOPE AND HELP FOR YOUR DIFFICULT TIMES

EDWARD D. ANDREWS

GOD WILL GET YOU THROUGH THIS

Hope and Help for Your Difficult Times

Edward D. Andrews

Christian Publishing House
Cambridge, Ohio

Copyright © 2023 Edward D. Andrews

All rights reserved. Except for brief quotations in articles, other publications, book reviews, and blogs, no part of this book may be reproduced in any manner without prior written permission from the publishers. For information, write, support@christianpublishers.org

Unless otherwise stated, Scripture quotations are from Updated American Standard Version (UASV) Copyright © 2022 by Christian Publishing House

GOD WILL GET YOU THROUGH THIS: Hope and Help for Your Difficult Times by Edward D. Andrews

ISBN-10: 1945757728

ISBN-13: 978-1945757723

Table of Contents

Book Description 9

Preface 10

Introduction 11

Chapter 1: Embracing God's Presence in Difficult Times .12

    1.1   Recognizing God's Everlasting Love 12

    1.2   Finding Comfort in God's Promises 13

    1.3   Leaning on God's Strength in Weakness 15

    1.4   Understanding God's Plan for Your Life 18

    1.5   Building a Personal Relationship with God 20

    1.6   Cultivating Gratitude Amidst Struggles 23

Chapter 2: Navigating Grief and Loss with God's Guidance 26

    2.1 The Healing Power of God's Love 26

    2.2 Finding Peace in God's Promises 29

    2.3 Seeking God's Comfort Through Prayer 31

    2.4 Letting Go and Trusting God's Timing 34

    2.5 Finding Hope and Renewal in God's Word 36

    2.6 The Role of Community and Fellowship 39

Chapter 3: Strengthening Your Marriage Through God's Wisdom 42

    3.1 The Foundation of a God-Centered Marriage 42

    3.2 Nurturing Love and Respect in Marriage 44

    3.3 Conflict Resolution: Turning to God for Guidance 47

    3.4 Growing Together Through Spiritual Practices 50

    3.5 The Power of Forgiveness and Reconciliation 53

    3.6 Supporting Each Other's Spiritual Growth 55

Chapter 4: Finding Hope in Illness and Health Challenges 58

    4.1 Trusting God's Plan for Your Health 58

    4.2 Seeking Strength and Peace an Accurate Understanding of God's Word 60

    4.3 Nurturing Your Spiritual Health Amidst Illness 62

    4.4 Finding Purpose and Meaning in Your Suffering 64

    4.5 Leaning on Your Faith Community for Support 66

    4.6 Embracing God's Healing and Restoration 68

Chapter 5: Overcoming Joblessness and Financial Struggles 71

    5.1 Trusting in God's Provision and Timing 71

    5.2 Cultivating a Heart of Contentment 73

    5.3 Seeking God's Wisdom for Financial Stewardship 75

    5.4 Harnessing the Power of Prayer in Job Hunting 77

    5.5 Building Resilience Through Faith and Perseverance 79

    5.6 Embracing New Opportunities with God's Guidance 81

Chapter 6: Alleviating Daily Stress with God's Help 84

    6.1 Developing a God-Centered Perspective on Stress 84

    6.2 Prioritizing Prayer and Meditation in Daily Life 86

    6.3 Learning to Surrender Control to God 87

    6.4 Implementing God's Wisdom in Time Management 89

    6.5 Cultivating a Spirit of Joy and Peace 91

    6.6 Strengthening Your Faith Through Life's Challenges 93

Chapter 7: Acquiring the Mind of Christ to Become Biblically Minded 96

    7.1 Understanding the Significance of the Mind of Christ 96

    7.2 Delving Deep into God's Word for Transformation 98

    7.3 Cultivating Humility, Love, and Servanthood 100

7.4 Embracing a Prayerful and Spirit-Led Life 102

7.5 Practicing Discernment and Applying Biblical Wisdom 104

7.6 Fostering Christlike Character and Virtues........................ 106

Chapter 8: Do Not Allow Your Circumstances to Control Your Life 109

8.1 Embracing God's Sovereignty Over Circumstances 109

8.2 Practicing Mindfulness and Acceptance........................... 111

8.3 Building Resilience Through Spiritual Growth 113

8.4 Cultivating a Positive and God-Centered Mindset.......... 114

8.5 Setting Healthy Boundaries and Priorities 116

8.6 Turning Challenges into Opportunities for Growth....... 118

Chapter 9: Cling to Your Faith Regardless of the Trial You Face... 121

9.1 Strengthening Your Trust in God's Plan 121

9.2 Harnessing the Power of Prayer During Trials 123

9.3 Learning from Biblical Examples of Perseverance 125

9.4 Nurturing Hope and Encouragement Through God's Word 127

9.5 Embracing the Role of Community and Support 129

9.6 Growing in Faith Through Every Season of Life............. 131

Chapter 10: Becoming a Spiritual Person and Maintaining Your Spirituality 134

10.1 Deepening Your Relationship with God 134

10.2 Developing a Consistent Prayer and Meditation Practice 137

10.3 Engaging in Regular Bible Study and Reflection........... 139

10.4 Prioritizing Worship and Spiritual Growth 144

10.5 Building Meaningful Connections with Fellow Believers 146

10.6 Serving Others and Demonstrating God's Love 148

Chapter 11: How to Deal with Anxiety 151

11.1 Acknowledging Anxiety and Turning to God................ 151

11.2 Implementing Spiritual Practices for Anxiety Relief..... 153

11.3 Trusting in God's Control and Sovereignty.................... 156

11.4 Developing a Balanced and God-Centered Lifestyle 158

11.5 Seeking Professional Help and Support When Needed 160

11.6 Encouraging Others and Sharing Your Testimony........ 162

BIBLIOGRAPHY **165**

Book Description

In the midst of life's challenges and struggles, it can be difficult to find solace and maintain our faith. "God Will Get You Through This" offers a beacon of hope and encouragement to those facing various trials, from grief and loss to financial hardship, health issues, and daily stress. This inspiring guide combines biblical wisdom, practical advice, and personal stories to help you not only survive but thrive during life's most trying times.

Discover the transformative power of God's love and presence as you delve into each chapter, exploring topics such as embracing God's guidance in difficult times, strengthening your marriage, and overcoming anxiety. Learn how to develop a strong, unwavering faith that will carry you through every trial, no matter how daunting. By acquiring the mind of Christ and becoming biblically minded, you can navigate life's challenges with grace, resilience, and a steadfast trust in God's plan.

This uplifting book offers a roadmap to spiritual growth and a deeper connection with God, empowering you to face your struggles head-on, armed with the assurance that God is always by your side. With its heartfelt guidance, "God Will Get You Through This" is an essential companion for anyone seeking hope, comfort, and strength in the face of life's most difficult moments.

… Edward D. Andrews

Preface

We live in a world filled with uncertainty and hardships, where it is not uncommon for individuals to find themselves grappling with overwhelming situations. As I have walked my own path and witnessed the struggles of others, it became increasingly apparent that there is a pressing need for a source of comfort, guidance, and hope to light the way during these difficult times. With this in mind, I set out to write "God Will Get You Through This," a book that not only serves as a lifeline for those who are drowning in their tribulations but also as a catalyst for spiritual growth and resilience.

In this book, I delve into the heart of what it means to be a Christian during life's darkest moments, offering valuable insights and practical advice grounded in biblical wisdom. Drawing from both personal experience and the experiences of others, I explore how our faith can be tested, yet ultimately strengthened, through adversity.

It is my hope that this book will provide you with the tools you need to face your challenges head-on and emerge stronger and more spiritually grounded than before. As you progress through each chapter, I invite you to reflect on your own experiences and consider how you can apply the lessons learned to your unique circumstances.

This journey is not only about finding solace amidst pain but also about discovering the transformative power of God's love and grace in every aspect of our lives. "God Will Get You Through This" is a testament to the enduring strength of our faith and a reminder that, even in the midst of our trials, we are never alone.

May this book be a source of hope, encouragement, and spiritual nourishment for you as you navigate your own path, and may it ultimately serve as a reminder that, with God's help, we can overcome anything that life may throw our way.

In His service and with His blessings,

Edward D. Andrews

Chief Translator of the Updated American Standard Version

Introduction

Each one of us, at some point in our lives, will face challenges that test our resilience, our faith, and our very understanding of the world around us. These trials come in many forms, from the loss of a loved one or a severe illness to financial struggles or the weight of daily stress. As we navigate these turbulent waters, we may find ourselves questioning our beliefs, our strength, and our ability to endure. It is during these moments that we must turn to the timeless wisdom of the Bible and the unwavering love of God for guidance and support.

This book, "God Will Get You Through This," is the culmination of my years of study, reflection, and personal experience in both the joys and the sorrows of life. Through each chapter, we will explore various aspects of our faith and how they can be applied to the challenges we face. Whether you are seeking comfort in the midst of grief, strength in the face of illness, guidance in your marriage, or relief from anxiety, this book offers practical and spiritual insights that will help you find hope and encouragement.

But this book is more than just a collection of advice and anecdotes. It is a testament to the enduring power of our faith and a reminder that, with God's help, we can overcome even the most difficult circumstances. As we delve into each chapter, we will reflect on the wisdom of the Bible, the examples of great men and women of faith, and the power of prayer and community in helping us endure and thrive.

It is my sincere hope that this book will serve as a source of inspiration, comfort, and guidance for those who are navigating difficult times. May it help you find the strength to persevere, the hope to endure, and the faith to trust in God's plan for your life.

Chapter 1: Embracing God's Presence in Difficult Times

1.1 Recognizing God's Everlasting Love

In difficult times, when we face challenges and hardships, it is essential to recognize and embrace God's everlasting love. While it is true that the Bible contains conditional statements, it also teaches that God's love is consistent and unwavering. This chapter aims to provide a comprehensive understanding of how to embrace God's presence in difficult times, acknowledging His love and the role it plays in our lives.

1. **Understanding God's Everlasting Love**

God's love is described as everlasting in various Bible verses (Jeremiah 31:3, Psalm 136). This indicates that His love is eternal, unchanging, and not bound by time. Although there may be conditions for certain aspects of our relationship with God, His love remains constant. This love provides the foundation for our faith and trust in Him, especially during trying times.

2. **The Role of Conditions in God's Love**

Conditions in the Bible serve as guidelines for living a righteous life, aligning ourselves with God's will, and nurturing our relationship with Him. Examples include the Ten Commandments, the teachings of Jesus, and other moral instructions. While these conditions outline how we can grow closer to God, they do not negate His love for us.

3. **Embracing God's Presence in Difficult Times**

When facing challenges, it is vital to draw strength from God's love and presence. Here are some ways to embrace His presence in difficult times:

a. **Prayer**: Communicate with God regularly through prayer, expressing your emotions, needs, and gratitude. This intimate connection can provide comfort and reassurance.

b. **Scripture Reading**: Immerse yourself in God's Word, finding passages that emphasize His love and promises. These verses can serve as reminders that He is always with you.

c. **Fellowship**: Engage with fellow believers, sharing your struggles and seeking encouragement from their experiences. This communal support can strengthen your faith.

d. **Worship**: Praise God through song, prayer, and meditation. This can help shift your focus from your circumstances to His everlasting love and presence.

e. **Trust**: Surrender your worries and fears to God, trusting that He is in control and will guide you through the difficult times.

4. **Experiencing God's Transformative Love**

In moments of hardship, God's love can transform our lives by providing hope, strength, and a renewed sense of purpose. As we embrace His presence, we can grow spiritually and develop a deeper relationship with Him.

Conclusion

Recognizing God's everlasting love is crucial when facing challenges and hardships. While the Bible contains conditional statements, these serve as guidelines for living a life aligned with God's will rather than negating His love. By embracing God's presence through prayer, scripture reading, fellowship, worship, and trust, we can experience His transformative love and find strength in difficult times.

1.2 Finding Comfort in God's Promises

God's promises hold immense significance for believers, providing hope, encouragement, and guidance throughout life's journey. It is essential to understand that while these promises are not absolutes, they still offer comfort and direction. In this comprehensive explanation, we will delve into the nature of God's promises and explore how to find comfort in them.

1. **The Nature of God's Promises**

While God's promises are not absolutes or guarantees, they serve as general principles that apply to our lives. Many promises are conditional, requiring our commitment, faith, and obedience. The Bible presents these promises as divine guidance, helping us navigate through various situations and circumstances.

2. **Types of God's Promises**

God's promises can be categorized into different types:

a. **Personal promises**: These are specific assurances given to individuals in the Bible, such as Abraham, Moses, and David. While these promises were intended for particular people, they can still inspire us and teach us about God's faithfulness.

b. **Conditional promises**: These promises rely on our actions or responses to God's guidance. Examples include the promise of blessings for obedience (Deuteronomy 28:1-14) and the assurance of forgiveness for those who repent (1 John 1:9).

c. **Unconditional promises**: These promises are based solely on God's faithfulness and do not depend on our actions. For instance, God's covenant with Noah after the flood (Genesis 9:8-17) demonstrates His commitment to preserving life on earth.

d. **General promises**: These are broad assurances that apply to all believers, such as the promise of God's presence (Matthew 28:20) and the gift of eternal life (John 3:16).

3. **Finding Comfort in God's Promises**

Understanding the general nature of God's promises helps us find comfort in the following ways:

a. **Recognize the Bigger Picture**: Accept that God's promises often have a broader context, transcending our immediate circumstances. Trust in His sovereignty and wisdom as He works in our lives.

b. **Cultivate Faith and Obedience**: Acknowledge that some promises are conditional and require our faithfulness. Strive to follow God's guidance and live a life aligned with His will.

c. **Embrace the Promises for All Believers**: Seek solace in the general promises that apply to all who believe, such as God's presence, His love, and the gift of eternal life.

d. **Reflect on Personal Experiences**: Recall times when God's promises have manifested in your life or the lives of others, reinforcing your trust in His faithfulness.

e. **Pray for Wisdom and Discernment**: Ask God to provide understanding and insight into His promises, enabling you to apply them effectively in your life.

Conclusion

Though God's promises are not absolutes, they provide comfort, hope, and guidance to believers. By understanding the general nature of these promises and recognizing the different types, we can find solace in them while navigating life's challenges. Cultivating faith and obedience, embracing promises meant for all believers, reflecting on personal experiences, and seeking wisdom and discernment through prayer can help us find comfort in God's promises.

1.3 Leaning on God's Strength in Weakness

Life presents us with numerous challenges, and during these moments of weakness, it is essential to lean on God's strength. In this comprehensive explanation, we will explore how to rely on divine support, drawing from biblical principles and practical steps to cultivate faith and resilience.

1. Understanding Weakness and God's Strength

Weakness can manifest in various forms, including physical, emotional, and spiritual difficulties. In these moments, we can draw strength from God, who is all-powerful, all-knowing, and ever-present. The Bible teaches us that God's strength is made perfect in our weakness (2 Corinthians 12:9), emphasizing the need to rely on Him when we feel incapable of handling life's challenges.

2. Biblical Examples of Leaning on God's Strength

Throughout the Bible, we find numerous examples of individuals who leaned on God's strength during their moments of weakness:

a. **Moses**: Despite his initial self-doubt and fear, Moses relied on God's strength to lead the Israelites out of Egypt (Exodus 3-4).

b. **David**: In his battle against Goliath, David trusted in God's power rather than his abilities, resulting in a victorious outcome (1 Samuel 17).

c. **Apostle Paul**: Paul experienced a "thorn in the flesh" that caused him great pain and suffering. He learned to rely on God's grace and strength, which enabled him to endure and persevere (2 Corinthians 12:7-10).

3. Practical Steps to Lean on God's Strength

a. **Acknowledge Your Weakness**: Admit your limitations and embrace your dependence on God. This humble recognition allows you to seek His strength in times of need.

b. **Pray for Strength**: Engage in regular prayer, asking God to provide His strength, guidance, and wisdom. Share your struggles and fears, trusting that He will empower you to overcome obstacles.

c. **Immerse Yourself in Scripture**: Study the Bible, focusing on passages that highlight God's strength and faithfulness. Use these verses as reminders of His power and presence in your life.

d. **Cultivate a Relationship with the Holy Spirit**: Invite the Holy Spirit to guide and empower you daily, allowing you to draw strength from the divine source within you.

e. **Surrender to God's Will**: Let go of control and trust in God's plans for your life. By surrendering your concerns to Him, you can experience His strength and support.

f. **Seek Fellowship**: Connect with other believers who can offer encouragement, prayer, and support. Sharing your experiences can help strengthen your faith and reliance on God.

4. **The Benefits of Leaning on God's Strength**

Relying on God's strength during moments of weakness offers numerous benefits:

a. **Spiritual Growth**: As we lean on God, our faith and relationship with Him deepen, leading to spiritual growth and maturity.

b. **Resilience**: Relying on divine strength helps us develop resilience, enabling us to face challenges and adversity with courage and confidence.

c. **Inner Peace**: Trusting in God's power and presence brings a sense of inner peace and assurance, even amidst difficult circumstances.

d. **Purpose and Direction**: Leaning on God's strength provides us with a sense of purpose and direction, guiding our decisions and actions.

Conclusion

Leaning on God's strength in weakness is a vital aspect of our spiritual journey. By acknowledging our limitations, praying for strength, immersing ourselves in Scripture, cultivating a relationship with the Holy Spirit, surrendering to God's will, and seeking fellowship, we can rely on divine support during life's challenges. This dependence on God's strength leads to spiritual growth, resilience, inner strength.

1.4 Understanding God's Plan for Your Life

God's plan for our lives encompasses our individual purpose, direction, and growth, shaped by His love and wisdom. Understanding and embracing this plan can be transformative and fulfilling, leading to a deeper relationship with God and a more meaningful existence. This comprehensive guide will explore how to discover and embrace God's plan for your life.

1. The Nature of God's Plan

God's plan for our lives is rooted in His love, wisdom, and desire for our well-being. It is characterized by the following attributes:

a. **Personal**: God's plan is tailored to each individual, taking into account our unique strengths, weaknesses, and circumstances.

b. **Dynamic**: Our understanding of God's plan may change and evolve over time as we grow spiritually and encounter new experiences.

c. **Purposeful**: God's plan is designed to help us fulfill our divine purpose, contributing to the greater good and enriching our lives.

d. **Redemptive**: God's plan can bring healing, restoration, and growth, even in the midst of challenges and setbacks.

2. Discovering God's Plan for Your Life

The process of understanding God's plan involves self-discovery, reflection, and discernment. Consider the following steps:

a. **Cultivate a Relationship with God**: Develop your spiritual connection through prayer, meditation, worship, and study of the Bible.

b. **Reflect on Your Talents and Passions**: Consider your unique gifts, interests, and abilities, recognizing how they align with God's plan.

c. **Seek Godly Wisdom**: Consult with trusted spiritual mentors, friends, and family members to gain insight and guidance.

d. **Discernment through Prayer**: Engage in regular, focused prayer, asking God for clarity and direction regarding His plan for your life.

e. **Learn from Life Experiences**: Reflect on your past and present experiences, identifying patterns, lessons, and opportunities for growth.

f. **Be Open to God's Guidance**: Maintain a receptive and humble attitude, being willing to change course or let go of preconceived notions.

3. Embracing God's Plan for Your Life

Once you have gained insight into God's plan, the next step is to embrace and follow it wholeheartedly:

a. **Surrender Your Will**: Submit to God's plan, relinquishing control and trusting in His guidance.

b. **Align Your Goals with God's Plan**: Set personal goals that align with your understanding of God's purpose for your life.

c. **Overcome Fear and Doubt**: Confront uncertainties and fears, relying on God's strength and assurance to overcome obstacles.

d. **Seek Accountability**: Share your understanding of God's plan with trusted friends or mentors, asking them to support and hold you accountable.

e. **Remain Adaptable**: Be willing to adjust your plans and expectations as you continue to grow and learn more about God's purpose for your life.

4. The Impact of Embracing God's Plan

Embracing God's plan for your life can have a profound impact on your spiritual journey and overall well-being:

a. **Spiritual Growth**: Following God's plan fosters spiritual development and a deeper relationship with Him.

b. **Fulfillment**: Aligning your life with God's purpose can bring a sense of satisfaction, meaning, and joy.

c. **Resilience**: Trusting in God's plan can provide strength and perseverance during difficult times.

d. **Positive Influence**: Living out God's plan can inspire others and contribute to the betterment of your community.

Conclusion

Understanding God's plan for your life is a vital aspect of spiritual growth and fulfillment. By cultivating a relationship with God, reflecting on your talents and passions, seeking wisdom, engaging in discernment through prayer, and learning the will of God, you will understand God's plan for your life.

1.5 Building a Personal Relationship with God

A personal relationship with God is at the core of the Christian faith. Developing and nurturing this connection allows for spiritual growth, a deeper understanding of God's love, and guidance throughout life's journey. This comprehensive guide will explore how to build a personal relationship with God, including practical steps and key elements to consider.

1. **The Foundation of a Personal Relationship with God**

A personal relationship with God is built upon the foundation of faith in Jesus Christ as Lord and Savior. This faith involves recognizing our need for forgiveness, accepting Christ's sacrifice on the cross, and committing our lives to following Him.

2. **Key Elements of a Personal Relationship with God**

Building a personal relationship with God requires active engagement in various spiritual practices, including:

a. **Prayer**: Regular communication with God through prayer is essential for cultivating intimacy and expressing our thoughts, emotions, and needs.

b. **Bible Study**: Reading and meditating on the Bible allows us to gain insight into God's nature, promises, and guidance.

c. **Worship**: Engaging in worship, both privately and within a community, helps us express our love and gratitude to God.

d. **Obedience**: Following God's commands and seeking to live according to His will is a vital aspect of deepening our relationship with Him.

e. **Holy Spirit**: Cultivating a relationship with the Holy Spirit enables us to receive guidance, strength, and spiritual gifts.

3. **Practical Steps to Building a Personal Relationship with God**

a. **Establish a Routine**: Set aside regular time for prayer, Bible study, and worship, creating a consistent routine that fosters spiritual growth.

b. **Journaling**: Record your thoughts, prayers, and reflections in a journal, helping to track your spiritual journey and deepen your understanding of God's work in your life.

c. **Seek Spiritual Mentorship**: Connect with a trusted spiritual mentor or friend who can offer guidance, encouragement, and accountability.

d. **Participate in a Faith Community**: Join a local church or small group where you can engage in fellowship, worship, and spiritual growth with fellow believers.

e. **Serve Others**: Embrace opportunities to serve others within your community, reflecting God's love and deepening your relationship with Him through acts of kindness and compassion.

4. **Overcoming Challenges in Building a Personal Relationship with God**

Developing a personal relationship with God may involve overcoming various challenges, such as:

a. **Busyness**: Prioritize your spiritual life, ensuring that you dedicate time and energy to nurturing your relationship with God.

b. **Doubt and Fear**: Address doubts and fears through prayer, seeking God's reassurance and guidance.

c. **Sin**: Confess and repent of your sins, seeking God's forgiveness and grace to help you grow in holiness and obedience.

d. **Distractions**: Minimize distractions during prayer and Bible study, creating an environment conducive to spiritual focus and contemplation.

5. The Impact of a Personal Relationship with God

Cultivating a personal relationship with God has numerous benefits, including:

a. **Spiritual Growth**: A deeper connection with God fosters growth in faith, character, and understanding of His will.

b. **Guidance and Wisdom**: Developing a personal relationship with God allows us to receive divine guidance and wisdom in our daily lives.

c. **Inner Peace and Joy**: Experiencing God's love and presence brings a sense of inner peace and joy, even during difficult times.

d. **Empowerment**: A personal relationship with God enables us to tap into divine strength, equipping us to face challenges and serve others.

Conclusion

Building a personal relationship with God is a lifelong journey that involves faith, commitment, and active engagement in various spiritual practices. By prioritizing prayer, Bible study, worship, obedience, and cultivating a personal relationship with God, you will find hope and help through your difficult times.

1.6 Cultivating Gratitude Amidst Struggles

Gratitude is a powerful practice that can significantly impact our well-being and resilience, even amidst struggles and difficulties. Cultivating gratitude during challenging times allows us to shift our perspective, focus on the positive aspects of our lives, and strengthen our connection with others and with God. This comprehensive guide will explore strategies for fostering thankfulness amidst struggles.

1. **Understanding the Importance of Gratitude**

Gratitude plays a vital role in our overall well-being and emotional health. Benefits of practicing gratitude include:

a. **Improved mental health**: Gratitude has been linked to increased happiness, reduced depression, and enhanced overall well-being.

b. **Increased resilience**: Thankfulness helps us cope with adversity, enabling us to bounce back from setbacks more quickly.

c. **Strengthened relationships**: Expressing gratitude promotes positive social interactions and deepens our connections with others.

d. **Enhanced spiritual growth**: Gratitude strengthens our relationship with God, fostering humility, trust, and dependence on His grace.

2. **Strategies for Cultivating Gratitude Amidst Struggles**

a. Reflect on past blessings: Recall positive experiences and moments of grace in your life, acknowledging the good things that have happened even in the midst of challenges.

b. **Keep a gratitude journal**: Regularly write down things you are grateful for, no matter how small or insignificant they may seem. This practice can help shift your focus from negative thoughts to a more positive perspective.

c. **Express gratitude to others**: Make an effort to thank those around you for their support, kindness, or presence in your life. This act of appreciation can improve your relationships and foster a sense of belonging.

d. **Practice mindfulness**: Engage in mindfulness exercises that help you focus on the present moment, cultivating an awareness of the blessings and beauty in your current circumstances.

e. **Pray with gratitude**: Incorporate thankfulness into your prayers, expressing gratitude to God for His love, provision, and guidance.

f. **Seek out positive stories and inspiration**: Surround yourself with uplifting content, such as inspiring books, films, or podcasts, that can encourage a grateful mindset.

3. Overcoming Obstacles to Gratitude

Cultivating gratitude amidst struggles may involve addressing various obstacles, such as:

a. **Negative thought patterns**: Challenge pessimistic thoughts and beliefs, replacing them with more positive and hopeful perspectives.

b. **Comparing yourself to others**: Resist the urge to compare your situation to others, focusing instead on the unique blessings in your own life.

c. **Dwelling on the past or future**: Embrace the present moment, acknowledging the good things that are happening right now, rather than fixating on past regrets or future worries.

4. The Impact of Gratitude on Coping with Struggles

Cultivating gratitude amidst challenges can lead to several positive outcomes:

a. **Alleviated emotional distress**: Gratitude can help reduce feelings of sadness, anxiety, and frustration, promoting emotional stability and well-being.

b. **A more balanced perspective**: Focusing on the positives in your life can help counterbalance the negative aspects, providing a more balanced and holistic view of your circumstances.

c. **Enhanced coping skills**: Gratitude can improve your ability to manage stress and adversity, increasing your resilience and adaptability.

d. **Strengthened faith**: Expressing gratitude to God can deepen your spiritual connection, enhancing your faith and reliance on His grace.

Conclusion

Cultivating gratitude amidst struggles is a transformative practice that can improve mental health, resilience, relationships, and spiritual growth. By reflecting on past blessings, keeping a gratitude journal, expressing gratitude to others, practicing mindfulness, praying with gratitude, and seeking out positive stories and inspiration, we can overcome obstacles and develop a more grateful mindset.

Chapter 2: Navigating Grief and Loss with God's Guidance

2.1 The Healing Power of God's Love

God's love is a profound source of healing and restoration for our physical, emotional, and spiritual well-being. As we open ourselves to this divine love, we can experience its transformative effects on our lives, relationships, and communities. In this comprehensive exploration, we will delve into the healing power of God's love, considering its different aspects and how it can impact our lives.

1. **The Nature of God's Love**

God's love is characterized by several attributes that contribute to its healing power:

a. **Unconditional**: God's love is not based on our performance, accomplishments, or merits; it is freely given and constant. However, God's love is certainly conditional. For example, Jesus said, "Not everyone who says to me, 'Lord, Lord,' will enter the kingdom of heaven, but **the one who does the will of my Father** who is in heaven." (Matt 7:21-23) This, of course, is a condition. The Bible is full of conditions that must be met or maintained in order to have a good standing with God.

b. **Sacrificial**: The depth of God's love is exemplified through the sacrifice of Jesus Christ on the cross, providing forgiveness and redemption for humanity.

c. **Compassionate**: God's love empathizes with our pain, suffering, and struggles, offering comfort and support.

d. **Transformative**: God's love has the power to change our hearts, minds, and lives, leading us to growth, healing, and restoration.

2. **The Healing Power of God's Love in Scripture**

Throughout the Bible, we find numerous examples of God's love bringing healing and transformation to individuals and communities:

a. **The Healing Ministry of Jesus**: Jesus demonstrated the healing power of God's love through His ministry, providing physical, emotional, and spiritual healing to those in need (e.g., Luke 8:43-48, Mark 2:1-12).

b. **God's Love for the Israelites**: God's love for His chosen people is evident throughout the Old Testament, offering guidance, protection, and healing amidst their trials and tribulations (e.g., Exodus 15:26, Psalm 147:3).

c. **The Apostle Paul**: Paul's encounter with God's love on the road to Damascus led to a radical transformation in his life, resulting in healing and a renewed purpose (Acts 9:1-19).

3. Experiencing the Healing Power of God's Love

To access the healing power of God's love, consider the following practices:

a. **Accept God's Love**: Open your heart and mind to receive God's love, believing in His unconditional and sacrificial affection for you.

b. **Cultivate a Relationship with God**: Engage in spiritual practices such as prayer, worship, and Bible study to deepen your connection with God and experience His love more fully.

c. **Embrace Forgiveness**: Accept God's forgiveness through Jesus Christ and extend forgiveness to yourself and others, allowing for emotional and spiritual healing.

d. **Seek Spiritual Support**: Connect with a faith community, spiritual mentor, or friends who can provide encouragement, prayer, and guidance in your journey toward healing.

e. **Practice Gratitude**: Focus on the blessings in your life, recognizing God's love in the midst of your circumstances.

f. **Share God's Love**: Extend love, kindness, and compassion to others, reflecting the healing power of God's love in your actions and relationships.

4. The Impact of the Healing Power of God's Love

Experiencing the healing power of God's love can lead to several positive outcomes:

a. **Emotional Healing**: God's love can bring comfort, peace, and healing to emotional wounds and traumas.

b. **Spiritual Healing**: Experiencing God's love can lead to a deeper relationship with Him, resulting in spiritual growth, renewal, and restoration.

c. **Physical Healing**: While not guaranteed, some individuals may experience physical healing as a manifestation of God's love and power.

d. **Relational Healing**: God's love can repair and restore broken relationships, fostering reconciliation and forgiveness.

e. **Community Healing**: As individuals and communities embrace God's love, they can work together to create environments of healing, support, and transformation. This collective healing can lead to positive change within families, neighborhoods, and society at large.

Conclusion

The healing power of God's love is a profound and transformative force that can bring comfort, restoration, and growth to our lives. By accepting God's love, cultivating a relationship with Him, embracing forgiveness, seeking spiritual support, practicing gratitude, and sharing God's love with others, we can experience the full impact of this divine healing. Through emotional, spiritual, physical, relational, and community healing, we can witness the transformative power of God's love and find hope, strength, and renewal amidst life's challenges.

2.2 Finding Peace in God's Promises

God's promises, as recorded in the Bible, serve as a source of hope, encouragement, and peace for believers. By understanding and trusting in these divine assurances, Christians can find strength and solace amidst life's challenges. This comprehensive exploration will delve into the biblical basis for finding peace in God's promises, drawing on conservative Christian interpretations.

1. **The Nature of God's Promises**

God's promises reflect His unchanging nature, steadfast love, and faithfulness. Key attributes of these promises include:

a. **Trustworthiness**: God's promises are reliable because they are rooted in His unchanging character (Numbers 23:19; Hebrews 6:18).

b. **Eternal**: God's promises extend beyond our earthly lives, reaching into eternity (Isaiah 40:8; Matthew 24:35).

c. **Conditional**: Some of God's promises require our obedience, faith, and commitment (John 15:10; Matthew 7:21).

2. **Biblical Examples of God's Promises**

The Bible is filled with numerous promises that provide comfort, guidance, and hope for believers. Some key examples include:

a. **Salvation**: God promises eternal life and forgiveness to those who believe in Jesus Christ (John 3:16; Acts 16:31).

b. **God's Presence**: God assures believers of His constant presence and guidance (Joshua 1:9; Isaiah 41:10).

c. **Peace**: God promises peace that surpasses all understanding to those who trust in Him (Philippians 4:6-7; Isaiah 26:3).

d. **Provision**: God commits to meeting our physical and emotional needs according to His riches in glory (Philippians 4:19; Matthew 6:31-33).

e. **Spiritual Growth**: God promises to sanctify and transform believers through the work of the Holy Spirit (Philippians 1:6; 2 Corinthians 3:18).

3. Finding Peace in God's Promises

To find peace in God's promises, believers can:

a. **Study Scripture**: Regularly read, meditate on, and memorize biblical passages that contain God's promises (Psalm 119:105; 2 Timothy 3:16-17).

b. **Pray**: Bring your concerns, fears, and needs to God in prayer, relying on His promises for comfort and guidance (1 Peter 5:7; Philippians 4:6).

c. **Trust in God's Faithfulness**: Cultivate trust in God's unchanging character and faithfulness, believing that He will fulfill His promises (Lamentations 3:22-23; Hebrews 10:23).

d. **Apply God's Promises**: Seek to live in alignment with God's promises by obeying His commands and walking in faith (James 1:22; John 14:15).

e. **Share God's Promises**: Encourage others with the promises of God, building up one another in faith and hope (1 Thessalonians 5:11; Hebrews 10:24-25).

4. The Impact of Finding Peace in God's Promises

Embracing God's promises and experiencing His peace can lead to several positive outcomes:

a. **Increased Faith**: Trusting in God's promises strengthens our faith and deepens our relationship with Him (Hebrews 11:6; James 1:2-4).

b. **Emotional Stability**: Relying on God's promises provides emotional stability during challenging times, offering comfort and hope (Psalm 46:1-3; 2 Corinthians 1:3-4).

c. **Resilience**: Leaning on God's promises enables us to withstand adversity and bounce back from setbacks more effectively (Romans 5:3-5; 2 Corinthians 4:8-9).

d. **Spiritual Growth**: By trusting and applying God's promises, we mature in our spiritual lives and become more Christ-like (Ephesians 4:15; Colossians 1:9-10).

e. **Strengthened Relationships**: Sharing God's promises with others fosters encouragement and support within our faith communities, promoting unity and love (1 Thessalonians 5:11; Ephesians 4:2-3).

Conclusion

Finding peace in God's promises is a central aspect of the Christian faith. These biblical assurances, grounded in God's unchanging nature, provide comfort, hope, and guidance for believers. By studying Scripture, praying, trusting in God's faithfulness, applying His promises, and sharing them with others, Christians can experience increased faith, emotional stability, resilience, spiritual growth, and strengthened relationships. In embracing God's promises, we can find peace and solace amidst life's challenges, deepening our relationship with our Creator and growing in our spiritual journey.

2.3 Seeking God's Comfort Through Prayer

Prayer is an essential aspect of the Christian faith, serving as a means of communication and connection with God. Through prayer, believers can seek comfort, guidance, and strength in the face of challenges and adversity. This comprehensive exploration will examine the biblical basis for seeking God's comfort through prayer, drawing on conservative Christian interpretations.

1. **The Importance of Prayer**

Prayer is a vital spiritual practice that helps to nurture our relationship with God. Key aspects of prayer include:

a. **Communication**: Prayer is a means of communicating with God, expressing our thoughts, feelings, and needs (Psalm 62:8; 1 Peter 5:7).

b. **Dependence**: Prayer demonstrates our reliance on God for strength, wisdom, and provision (Proverbs 3:5-6; Philippians 4:6).

c. **Worship**: Through prayer, we can worship and praise God, acknowledging His attributes and expressing gratitude for His blessings (Psalm 95:1-2; Philippians 4:4).

d. **Transformation**: Prayer has the power to change our hearts, minds, and circumstances, aligning our will with God's (Romans 12:2; James 5:16).

2. Biblical Examples of Seeking Comfort Through Prayer

The Bible contains numerous examples of individuals who sought God's comfort through prayer during difficult times:

a. **King David**: David often turned to prayer for comfort and guidance during his struggles, as seen throughout the Psalms (e.g., Psalm 23; Psalm 61).

b. **Jesus Christ**: Jesus sought comfort and strength from the Father through prayer, especially during challenging moments, such as in the Garden of Gethsemane (Matthew 26:36-44; Luke 22:39-46).

c. **Apostle Paul**: Paul consistently prayed for strength, wisdom, and comfort amid trials, as well as for the well-being of fellow believers (Ephesians 1:15-23; Philippians 1:3-11).

3. Seeking God's Comfort Through Prayer: Practical Steps

To seek God's comfort through prayer, consider the following practices:

a. **Be Honest**: Approach God with authenticity, expressing your feelings, concerns, and needs openly (Psalm 62:8; 1 John 5:14).

b. **Pray Regularly**: Develop a consistent prayer life, setting aside specific times each day to pray and maintain an ongoing conversation with God (1 Thessalonians 5:17; Daniel 6:10).

c. **Use Scripture**: Incorporate Scripture into your prayers, drawing on God's promises and biblical examples to inform and enrich your prayer life (Psalm 119:105; John 15:7).

d. **Pray with Others**: Seek comfort and support through prayer with fellow believers, sharing burdens and encouraging one another (Matthew 18:19-20; James 5:16).

e. **Practice Listening**: Cultivate a posture of listening during prayer, being open to God's guidance, and the Holy Spirit's leading (John 10:27; Isaiah 30:21).

4. The Impact of Seeking Comfort Through Prayer

Embracing prayer as a means of seeking God's comfort can lead to several positive outcomes:

a. **Spiritual Growth**: Prayer nurtures our relationship with God, fostering spiritual maturity and development (Colossians 4:2; Ephesians 6:18).

b. **Emotional Healing**: Prayer can bring emotional healing and peace, as we share our burdens with God and receive His comfort (Psalm 34:18; Isaiah 57:18).

c. **Guidance and Wisdom**: Through prayer, we can receive divine guidance and wisdom, helping us navigate life's challenges and make sound decisions (James 1:5; Proverbs 3:5-6).

d. **Increased Faith**: Engaging in prayer can strengthen our faith, as we witness God's faithfulness in answering our prayers and providing comfort (Matthew 21:22; Hebrews 11:6).

e. **Strengthened Relationships**: Praying with and for others fosters unity, support, and love within our faith communities, promoting deeper connections and mutual encouragement (Colossians 1:9-12; 1 Thessalonians 5:11).

Conclusion

Seeking God's comfort through prayer is a vital aspect of the Christian faith, providing a means of communication and connection with our Creator. As we approach God with honesty, pray regularly, use Scripture, pray with others, and practice listening, we can experience spiritual growth, emotional healing, guidance, increased faith, and strengthened relationships. By engaging in prayer during life's challenges, believers can find solace, hope, and strength in the arms of a loving God who is eager to provide comfort and guidance.

2.4 Letting Go and Trusting God's Timing

Trusting in God's timing is an essential aspect of the Christian faith, requiring believers to surrender control and place their confidence in God's perfect plan for their lives. This comprehensive exploration will examine the biblical basis for letting go and trusting in God's timing, drawing on conservative Christian interpretations.

1. **The Sovereignty of God**

Central to trusting in God's timing is the understanding of His sovereignty, which encompasses:

a. **God's control**: God exercises ultimate control over all aspects of creation, history, and human lives (Psalm 115:3; Ephesians 1:11).

b. **God's wisdom**: God possesses perfect wisdom and understanding, enabling Him to make the best decisions for our lives (Romans 11:33; Isaiah 55:8-9).

c. **God's love**: God's love for His children ensures that His timing and plans are always for their ultimate good (Romans 8:28; Jeremiah 29:11).

2. **Biblical Examples of Trusting God's Timing**

The Bible contains numerous examples of individuals who trusted in God's timing, even in the face of uncertainty or delay:

a. **Abraham and Sarah**: Despite their advanced age, Abraham and Sarah trusted in God's promise of a child and experienced the fulfillment of His plan in His perfect timing (Genesis 21:1-7; Hebrews 11:11-12).

b. **Joseph**: After being sold into slavery and imprisoned, Joseph continued to trust in God's timing, ultimately witnessing God's plan unfold as he became a powerful leader in Egypt (Genesis 45:4-8; 50:20).

c. **Moses**: Moses spent 40 years in the wilderness before God called him to lead the Israelites out of Egypt, demonstrating the importance of trusting in God's timing (Exodus 3:1-10; Acts 7:23-30).

3. Letting Go and Trusting God's Timing: Practical Steps

To let go and trust in God's timing, consider the following practices:

a. **Pray**: Seek God's guidance through prayer, asking for wisdom, patience, and faith to trust in His timing (Philippians 4:6-7; James 1:5).

b. **Study Scripture**: Read and meditate on biblical passages that emphasize God's sovereignty, timing, and faithfulness (Psalm 37:7; Ecclesiastes 3:1).

c. **Cultivate Patience**: Develop patience and perseverance, understanding that God's timing may differ from our expectations (Romans 5:3-4; Hebrews 10:36).

d. **Surrender Control**: Release the desire for control and submit to God's will, acknowledging His authority and wisdom in our lives (Proverbs 3:5-6; Matthew 16:24-25).

e. **Encourage One Another**: Share experiences and insights with fellow believers, providing mutual support and encouragement in trusting God's timing (1 Thessalonians 5:11; Hebrews 10:24-25).

4. The Impact of Trusting God's Timing

Embracing trust in God's timing can lead to several positive outcomes:

a. **Increased Faith**: Trusting in God's timing deepens our faith, as we witness His faithfulness and perfect plan unfold in our lives (2 Corinthians 5:7; Hebrews 11:1).

b. **Peace and Contentment**: Letting go of control and trusting in God's timing brings peace and contentment, as we rest in His sovereign care (Philippians 4:6-7; Isaiah 26:3).

c. **Spiritual Growth**: By trusting in God's timing, we develop patience, perseverance, and other spiritual virtues that contribute to our spiritual maturity (James 1:2-4; 2 Peter 1:5-8).

d. **Reduced Anxiety**: Surrendering control and relying on God's timing can alleviate anxiety and worry, as we acknowledge that our lives are in His capable hands (Matthew 6:25-34; 1 Peter 5:7).

e. **Strengthened Relationships**: Trusting in God's timing within our faith communities fosters unity, understanding, and mutual encouragement, promoting stronger relationships among believers (Ephesians 4:2-3; Colossians 3:12-14).

Conclusion

Letting go and trusting in God's timing is a vital aspect of the Christian faith, requiring believers to relinquish control and place their confidence in God's perfect plan. By understanding His sovereignty, studying Scripture, praying, cultivating patience, surrendering control, and encouraging one another, Christians can experience increased faith, peace, contentment, spiritual growth, reduced anxiety, and strengthened relationships. Trusting in God's timing allows believers to rest in the knowledge that God's love, wisdom, and sovereignty will guide their lives according to His perfect plan and timing.

2.5 Finding Hope and Renewal in God's Word

God's Word, as revealed in the Bible, is a powerful source of hope and renewal for believers. It offers guidance, encouragement, and inspiration, equipping Christians to navigate life's challenges and grow in their relationship with God. This comprehensive exploration will examine the biblical basis for finding hope and renewal in God's Word, drawing on conservative Christian interpretations.

1. **The Authority and Power of God's Word**

The Bible is God's inspired and authoritative Word, serving as the ultimate source of truth and wisdom for believers:

a. **Divine Inspiration**: The Bible is inspired by the Holy Spirit and serves as God's revelation to humanity (2 Timothy 3:16; 2 Peter 1:20-21).

b. **Truth**: God's Word is the ultimate source of truth, providing guidance and clarity in a world filled with confusion and uncertainty (Psalm 119:160; John 17:17).

c. **Life-Changing Power**: The Bible has the power to transform lives, bringing hope, renewal, and spiritual growth (Hebrews 4:12; Isaiah 55:10-11).

2. Biblical Examples of Hope and Renewal in God's Word

The Bible is filled with examples of individuals who found hope and renewal through their engagement with God's Word:

a. **King David**: David found comfort, hope, and renewal in God's Word during times of adversity, as expressed in the Psalms (e.g., Psalm 19:7-14; Psalm 119:49-50).

b. **Prophet Jeremiah**: Jeremiah drew hope and strength from God's Word in the midst of his trials and suffering (Jeremiah 15:16; Lamentations 3:21-24).

c. **Apostle Paul**: Paul relied on the Scriptures to sustain him during his persecutions, encouraging others with the truths found in God's Word (Romans 15:4; 2 Timothy 3:14-17).

3. Finding Hope and Renewal in God's Word: Practical Steps

To find hope and renewal in God's Word, consider the following practices:

a. **Regular Bible Reading**: Develop a consistent routine of reading and meditating on Scripture to encounter God's truth daily (Joshua 1:8; Psalm 1:2-3).

b. **Memorization**: Memorize key verses and passages, enabling you to draw on the truths of God's Word in times of need (Psalm 119:11; Colossians 3:16).

c. **Study**: Engage in in-depth study of the Bible to gain a deeper understanding of its message and application to your life (Acts 17:11; 2 Timothy 2:15).

d. **Prayer**: Pray for the Holy Spirit's guidance as you read and study Scripture, asking God to reveal His truth and provide hope and renewal (John 14:26; James 1:5).

e. **Apply the Word**: Apply the principles and truths found in Scripture to your daily life, allowing God's Word to shape your thoughts, actions, and decisions (James 1:22-25; Romans 12:2).

4. The Impact of Finding Hope and Renewal in God's Word

Embracing God's Word as a source of hope and renewal can lead to several positive outcomes:

a. **Spiritual Growth**: Engaging with Scripture fosters spiritual maturity and deepens your relationship with God (1 Peter 2:2; Colossians 3:16).

b. **Renewed Mind**: God's Word has the power to renew your mind, transforming your thoughts and perspectives (Romans 12:2; Ephesians 4:23).

c. **Encouragement and Comfort**: Scripture provides encouragement and comfort during difficult times, reminding believers of God's promises and faithfulness (2 Corinthians 1:3-4; Psalm 119:50).

d. **Guidance and Wisdom**: Through engagement with God's Word, Christians gain wisdom and guidance for navigating life's challenges (Psalm 119:105; Proverbs 3:5-6).

e. **Strengthened Community**: As believers collectively immerse themselves in Scripture, they experience unity, mutual encouragement, and a shared understanding of God's truth (Colossians 3:16; Hebrews 10:24-25).

Conclusion

Finding hope and renewal in God's Word is essential for believers, as Scripture serves as a reliable source of truth, guidance, and inspiration. By engaging in regular Bible reading, memorization, study, prayer, and application, Christians can experience spiritual growth, renewed minds, encouragement, comfort, guidance, wisdom, and strengthened community. Embracing God's Word as a powerful tool for hope and renewal enables believers to navigate life's challenges with confidence, resting in the promises and faithfulness of God.

2.6 The Role of Community and Fellowship

Community and fellowship play a significant role in the Christian faith, providing believers with support, encouragement, and opportunities for spiritual growth. This comprehensive exploration will examine the biblical basis for the importance of community and fellowship, drawing on conservative Christian interpretations.

1. The Biblical Foundation for Community and Fellowship

The Bible emphasizes the importance of community and fellowship among believers:

a. **Creation**: From the beginning, God created humans to be in relationship with one another, recognizing that it was not good for man to be alone (Genesis 2:18).

b. **Early Church**: The early Christian church modeled the importance of fellowship by regularly gathering for prayer, breaking of bread, and sharing of possessions (Acts 2:42-47).

c. **Body of Christ**: The New Testament frequently uses the metaphor of the body to describe the church, emphasizing the interconnectedness of believers and their reliance on one another (1 Corinthians 12:12-27; Romans 12:4-5).

2. The Importance of Community and Fellowship

Community and fellowship are vital aspects of the Christian faith for several reasons:

a. **Spiritual Growth**: Believers grow spiritually through encouragement, accountability, and the sharing of insights within a community of faith (Hebrews 10:24-25; Proverbs 27:17).

b. **Support and Encouragement**: Christian community provides a network of support and encouragement, helping believers to navigate life's challenges (Galatians 6:2; 1 Thessalonians 5:11).

c. **Worship and Prayer**: Gathering with other believers allows for corporate worship and prayer, strengthening the faith of the community and glorifying God (Ephesians 5:19-20; Matthew 18:20).

d. **Service and Outreach**: Fellowship enables believers to work together in serving their community and sharing the Gospel, fulfilling the Great Commission (Matthew 28:18-20; Acts 1:8).

3. Building and Maintaining Christian Community

To establish and maintain a strong Christian community, consider the following practices:

a. **Regular Gatherings**: Attend worship services, Bible studies, and other gatherings regularly to foster relationships and maintain a sense of unity (Hebrews 10:25; Acts 2:46).

b. **Openness and Vulnerability**: Cultivate an environment of openness and vulnerability, allowing members to share their struggles, doubts, and joys (James 5:16; Galatians 6:2).

c. **Hospitality and Inclusivity**: Welcome newcomers and create an inclusive atmosphere that fosters diversity and unity (Romans 15:7; 1 Peter 4:9).

d. **Servant Leadership**: Encourage and practice servant leadership within the community, modeling Christ's example of humility and service (Matthew 20:26-28; Philippians 2:3-5).

e. **Conflict Resolution**: Address conflicts and disagreements with grace, forgiveness, and a commitment to reconciliation (Matthew 18:15-17; Ephesians 4:25-27).

4. The Impact of Christian Community and Fellowship

Strong Christian communities and fellowship can lead to several positive outcomes:

a. **Strengthened Faith**: Engaging in community and fellowship deepens individual faith and fosters collective spiritual growth (Ephesians 4:15-16; Colossians 2:6-7).

b. **Emotional and Spiritual Support**: Believers benefit from the emotional and spiritual support provided by their faith community during times of hardship (2 Corinthians 1:3-4; 1 Thessalonians 4:13-18).

c. **Empowered Service**: Christian communities can more effectively serve their local communities and share the Gospel when working together, drawing upon the unique gifts and talents of each member (1 Corinthians 12:4-11; Ephesians 4:11-13).

d. **Unity and Reconciliation**: Engaging in fellowship and community helps to promote unity and reconciliation, breaking down barriers and fostering understanding among diverse groups of believers (Ephesians 2:14-16; Colossians 3:12-14).

e. **Edification of the Church**: A strong Christian community benefits the overall health and growth of the church, as believers are equipped to serve and build up the body of Christ (Ephesians 4:12-16; 1 Thessalonians 5:11).

Conclusion

Community and fellowship play an essential role in the Christian faith, providing believers with opportunities for spiritual growth, support, encouragement, worship, prayer, and service. By prioritizing regular gatherings, openness, vulnerability, hospitality, inclusivity, servant leadership, and conflict resolution, Christians can build and maintain strong communities that foster deepened faith, emotional and spiritual support, empowered service, unity, and edification of the church. Embracing the biblical call to community and fellowship enables believers to live out their faith more fully and effectively, reflecting the love and unity that God desires for His people.

Chapter 3: Strengthening Your Marriage Through God's Wisdom

3.1 The Foundation of a God-Centered Marriage

A God-centered marriage, rooted in biblical principles, offers a strong foundation for a lasting, fulfilling, and joyful union. This comprehensive exploration will examine the biblical basis for building a God-centered marriage, drawing on conservative Christian interpretations.

1. **The Biblical Foundation for Marriage**

The Bible provides a clear framework for marriage, emphasizing its importance, purpose, and divine origin:

a. **Creation**: Marriage was instituted by God at creation, signifying the complementary relationship between a man and a woman (Genesis 2:18-24).

b. **Covenant**: Marriage is a covenantal relationship, reflecting the commitment, faithfulness, and love that exists between God and His people (Malachi 2:14; Ephesians 5:25-27).

c. **Procreation**: One of the purposes of marriage is procreation, providing a stable environment for raising children in the knowledge and love of God (Genesis 1:28; Psalm 127:3-5).

d. **Unity**: Marriage is a union between a man and a woman, in which they become "one flesh" and share a deep, intimate bond (Genesis 2:24; Matthew 19:4-6).

2. **Principles for Building a God-Centered Marriage**

To build a God-centered marriage, consider the following biblical principles:

a. **Christ as the Foundation**: Place Christ at the center of your marriage, seeking to grow in your relationship with Him individually and as a couple (Colossians 3:17; Ephesians 5:21).

b. **Love**: Demonstrate selfless, sacrificial love toward your spouse, reflecting the love Christ has for the church (Ephesians 5:25; 1 Corinthians 13:4-7).

c. **Respect and Submission**: Wives are encouraged to respect and submit to their husbands, while husbands are called to love their wives as Christ loved the church (Ephesians 5:22-33; Colossians 3:18-19).

d. **Communication**: Cultivate open, honest, and loving communication, seeking to resolve conflicts and misunderstandings with grace and forgiveness (Ephesians 4:25-27, 29; James 1:19).

e. **Spiritual Growth**: Pursue spiritual growth together by engaging in regular prayer, Bible study, and worship, both individually and as a couple (Deuteronomy 6:6-7; 1 Peter 3:7).

3. Nurturing a God-Centered Marriage

To nurture a God-centered marriage, consider these practices:

a. **Prioritize Time Together**: Spend quality time together to build intimacy, trust, and connection (Song of Solomon 7:10-12; Ecclesiastes 9:9).

b. **Encourage One Another**: Offer encouragement, support, and affirmation to your spouse, helping them to grow in their faith and relationship with God (1 Thessalonians 5:11; Hebrews 10:24-25).

c. **Serve Together**: Engage in acts of service and ministry as a couple, using your unique gifts and talents to further God's kingdom (1 Peter 4:10-11; Galatians 6:9-10).

d. **Cultivate a Supportive Community**: Build relationships with other Christian couples, seeking their guidance, encouragement, and accountability (Proverbs 27:17; Hebrews 10:24-25).

4. The Impact of a God-Centered Marriage

A God-centered marriage can result in numerous positive outcomes:

a. **Spiritual Growth**: Couples who prioritize their relationship with God and one another will experience spiritual growth, both individually and as a couple (2 Peter 3:18; Ecclesiastes 4:9-12).

b. **Stronger Bond**: A God-centered marriage fosters a stronger bond between spouses, built on trust, love, and a shared commitment to Christ (Ecclesiastes 4:12; 1 Corinthians 13:4-7).

c. **Resilience**: Couples grounded in their faith are better equipped to navigate life's challenges and hardships, drawing strength from their relationship with God and one another (Isaiah 40:31; Philippians 4:13).

d. **Lasting Legacy**: A God-centered marriage provides a positive example for children and future generations, teaching them the importance of placing Christ at the center of their lives and relationships (Deuteronomy 6:6-7; Psalm 78:4-7).

Conclusion

The foundation of a God-centered marriage is rooted in biblical principles and provides the basis for a lasting, fulfilling, and joyful union. By placing Christ at the center of their marriage, demonstrating love, respect, and submission, cultivating open communication, pursuing spiritual growth, and nurturing their relationship through quality time, encouragement, service, and supportive community, couples can build and maintain a strong, God-centered marriage. This type of marriage fosters spiritual growth, a stronger bond between spouses, resilience in the face of challenges, and a lasting legacy for future generations, reflecting the beauty and purpose of God's design for marriage.

3.2 Nurturing Love and Respect in Marriage

Love and respect are foundational elements in a healthy, God-centered marriage. Nurturing these qualities helps to create a thriving, supportive, and fulfilling relationship between spouses. This comprehensive exploration will examine the biblical basis for nurturing love and respect in marriage, drawing on conservative Christian interpretations.

1. The Biblical Basis for Love and Respect in Marriage

The Bible provides clear guidance on the importance of love and respect within marriage:

a. **Husbands**: Husbands are called to love their wives with a selfless, sacrificial love, reflecting Christ's love for the church (Ephesians 5:25; Colossians 3:19).

b. **Wives**: Wives are instructed to respect and submit to their husbands, acknowledging their leadership within the family (Ephesians 5:22-24; Colossians 3:18).

c. **Mutual Submission**: Both husbands and wives are called to submit to one another out of reverence for Christ, emphasizing the importance of mutual love and respect (Ephesians 5:21).

2. Nurturing Love and Respect in Marriage

To nurture love and respect in your marriage, consider these biblical principles:

a. **Intentionality**: Make a conscious effort to demonstrate love and respect to your spouse daily, recognizing that these qualities require ongoing effort and commitment (1 Corinthians 16:14; Romans 12:10).

b. **Forgiveness and Grace**: Practice forgiveness and extend grace to your spouse, acknowledging that both partners are imperfect and will make mistakes (Colossians 3:13; Ephesians 4:32).

c. **Servanthood**: Emulate Christ's example of servanthood by putting your spouse's needs above your own (Philippians 2:3-4; John 13:14-15).

d. **Communication**: Cultivate open, honest, and loving communication, ensuring that your words and actions convey love and respect (Proverbs 15:1; Ephesians 4:29).

3. Practical Steps for Fostering Love and Respect

To foster love and respect in your marriage, consider implementing these practical steps:

a. **Spend Quality Time Together**: Prioritize spending quality time with your spouse, focusing on building intimacy, trust, and connection (Song of Solomon 7:10-12; Ecclesiastes 9:9).

b. **Express Gratitude**: Regularly express gratitude and appreciation for your spouse, acknowledging their efforts, sacrifices, and contributions to the relationship (1 Thessalonians 5:18; Colossians 3:15).

c. **Offer Encouragement**: Encourage your spouse in their personal, spiritual, and professional growth, supporting their goals and dreams (1 Thessalonians 5:11; Hebrews 10:24-25).

d. **Pray Together**: Make prayer a central part of your relationship, seeking God's guidance, wisdom, and blessing for your marriage (Matthew 18:19-20; James 5:16).

4. The Impact of Love and Respect in Marriage

When love and respect are nurtured within a marriage, several positive outcomes result:

a. **Stronger Bond**: A marriage built on love and respect fosters a stronger bond between spouses, creating a deep sense of intimacy, trust, and unity (Genesis 2:24; Proverbs 18:22).

b. **Emotional and Spiritual Support**: Couples who prioritize love and respect provide emotional and spiritual support to one another, offering encouragement and understanding during challenging times (Ecclesiastes 4:9-12; Galatians 6:2).

c. **Spiritual Growth**: A marriage grounded in love and respect fosters spiritual growth for both individuals and the couple as a whole, as they learn to embody Christ-like qualities and deepen their relationship with God (2 Peter 3:18; Ephesians 4:15-16).

d. **Positive Influence**: Couples who nurture love and respect within their marriage serve as a positive influence on their children, extended family, friends, and community, reflecting the beauty of God's design for marriage (Matthew 5:16; 1 Peter 3:1-2).

Conclusion

Nurturing love and respect in marriage is essential for creating a healthy, thriving, and fulfilling relationship between spouses. By following biblical guidance, implementing practical steps, and maintaining intentionality, forgiveness, servanthood, and open communication, couples can foster love and respect within their marriage. The impact of nurturing these qualities results in a stronger bond, emotional and spiritual support, spiritual growth, and a positive influence on those around them. Embracing the biblical call to love and respect in marriage enables couples to experience the fullness of God's plan for their relationship, ultimately reflecting His love, grace, and wisdom.

3.3 Conflict Resolution: Turning to God for Guidance

Conflict is an inevitable part of life, even within Christian relationships and marriages. However, by turning to God for guidance, we can resolve conflicts in a way that honors Him and fosters growth and reconciliation. This comprehensive exploration will examine the biblical basis for seeking God's guidance in conflict resolution, drawing on conservative Christian interpretations.

1. **The Biblical Basis for Seeking God's Guidance in Conflict Resolution**

The Bible offers clear guidance on resolving conflicts and seeking God's wisdom in difficult situations:

a. **Wisdom**: God is the source of all wisdom, and turning to Him for guidance can help us navigate conflict with grace, discernment, and understanding (James 1:5; Proverbs 2:6).

b. **Humility**: Approaching conflict with humility allows us to recognize our own shortcomings and be open to correction (Proverbs 15:33; Philippians 2:3-4).

c. **Reconciliation**: God desires reconciliation and peace among His people, encouraging us to resolve conflicts and pursue unity (Matthew 5:23-24; 2 Corinthians 5:18-19).

2. Principles for Conflict Resolution with God's Guidance

To resolve conflicts with God's guidance, consider these biblical principles:

a. **Prayer**: Seek God's wisdom and direction through prayer, asking Him to help you discern the right course of action (Philippians 4:6-7; James 1:5).

b. **Listening**: Practice active listening, giving your full attention to the other person's perspective without interrupting or formulating your response (James 1:19; Proverbs 18:13).

c. **Speak the Truth in Love**: Address the issue honestly and respectfully, sharing your thoughts and feelings while maintaining a loving and gentle tone (Ephesians 4:15, 25-27).

d. **Forgiveness**: Be willing to forgive and extend grace, recognizing that we are all imperfect and in need of God's forgiveness (Ephesians 4:32; Colossians 3:13).

3. Practical Steps for Resolving Conflict with God's Guidance

To resolve conflicts with God's guidance, consider implementing these practical steps:

a. **Begin with Prayer**: Start by praying together, asking for God's wisdom and guidance as you discuss the issue at hand (Matthew 18:19-20; 1 Thessalonians 5:17).

b. **Clarify the Issue**: Clearly and calmly explain the issue from your perspective, seeking to understand the other person's viewpoint as well (Proverbs 18:2; James 1:19).

c. **Find Common Ground**: Identify areas of agreement and shared values, working together to find a mutually acceptable resolution (Philippians 2:2; Romans 12:16).

d. **Develop a Plan**: Collaboratively develop a plan for moving forward, including specific steps for addressing the issue and avoiding future conflicts (Ecclesiastes 4:9-10; Romans 15:5-6).

4. The Impact of Seeking God's Guidance in Conflict Resolution

When we seek God's guidance in conflict resolution, we can experience several positive outcomes:

a. **Personal Growth**: Resolving conflicts in a godly manner fosters personal growth and maturity, as we learn to embody Christ-like qualities such as humility, patience, and forgiveness (James 1:2-4; Romans 5:3-5).

b. **Strengthened Relationships**: Working through conflicts with God's guidance can lead to stronger, more resilient relationships built on trust, understanding, and grace (Proverbs 27:17; Colossians 3:12-14).

c. **Peace and Unity**: Seeking God's guidance in conflict resolution promotes peace and unity within our relationships, families, and communities, reflecting the harmony that God desires for His people (Romans 14:19; Colossians 3:15).

d. **Testimony**: Resolving conflicts with God's guidance serves as a powerful testimony to others, demonstrating the transformative power of Christ's love and the wisdom of His teachings (Matthew 5:16; 1 Peter 2:12).

Conclusion

Turning to God for guidance in conflict resolution is essential for navigating disagreements and fostering growth, reconciliation, and unity. By following biblical principles and implementing practical steps, we can resolve conflicts in a way that honors God and strengthens our relationships. The impact of seeking God's guidance in conflict resolution includes personal growth, strengthened relationships, peace and unity, and a powerful testimony to others. By embracing the biblical call to seek God's guidance in resolving conflicts, we can experience the fullness of God's wisdom, grace, and love in our relationships and daily lives.

3.4 Growing Together Through Spiritual Practices

Spiritual practices are essential for individual growth and cultivating a strong relationship with God. They are also crucial for couples, families, and communities to grow together in their faith. This comprehensive exploration will examine the biblical basis for growing together through spiritual practices, drawing on conservative Christian interpretations.

1. **The Biblical Basis for Growing Together Through Spiritual Practices**

The Bible emphasizes the importance of spiritual practices in nurturing our relationships with God and others:

a. **Prayer**: Scripture encourages believers to pray individually and with others, seeking God's guidance and strength (1 Thessalonians 5:17; Matthew 18:19-20).

b. **Studying the Word**: The Bible instructs Christians to study God's Word, both individually and collectively, to gain wisdom and understanding (2 Timothy 3:16-17; Acts 17:11).

c. **Fellowship**: Believers are called to gather in fellowship, encouraging and supporting one another in their faith (Hebrews 10:24-25; Acts 2:42).

d. **Worship**: Christians are invited to worship God together, expressing gratitude and praise for His goodness and love (Psalm 95:1-2; Colossians 3:16).

2. **Spiritual Practices for Growing Together**

To grow together through spiritual practices, consider incorporating the following into your shared faith journey:

a. **Praying Together**: Establish a regular time for prayer with your spouse, family, or community, sharing requests and thanksgivings (Matthew 18:19-20; James 5:16).

b. **Studying the Bible Together**: Engage in regular Bible study, discussing passages, asking questions, and applying biblical truths to daily life (Acts 17:11; 2 Timothy 2:15).

c. **Worshiping Together**: Participate in corporate worship, joining with others in praise, prayer, and reflection (Hebrews 12:28; Psalm 100:1-2).

d. **Serving Together**: Seek opportunities to serve others as a couple, family, or community, reflecting Christ's example of love and compassion (Galatians 5:13; 1 Peter 4:10).

3. Practical Steps for Implementing Spiritual Practices

To implement spiritual practices for growing together, consider these practical steps:

a. **Create a Routine**: Develop a routine that incorporates spiritual practices, allowing time for prayer, Bible study, worship, and service (Ephesians 5:15-16; Psalm 90:12).

b. **Establish Accountability**: Hold one another accountable for participating in spiritual practices, offering encouragement and support (Ecclesiastes 4:9-12; Proverbs 27:17).

c. **Be Adaptable**: Recognize that life circumstances may change, requiring flexibility in your spiritual practices. Adapt your routine as needed while maintaining your commitment to growth (Philippians 4:11-13; James 1:2-4).

d. **Encourage Others**: Invite others to join you in spiritual practices, providing a supportive and inclusive environment for growth (1 Thessalonians 5:11; Romans 15:5-6).

4. The Impact of Growing Together Through Spiritual Practices

Growing together through spiritual practices offers several benefits:

a. **Strengthened Faith**: Engaging in spiritual practices deepens and strengthens individual and collective faith, fostering a closer relationship with God (Ephesians 4:15-16; Colossians 2:6-7).

b. **Enhanced Relationships**: Shared spiritual practices nurture a sense of unity and shared purpose within couples, families, and communities (1 Corinthians 1:10; Ephesians 4:3).

c. **Spiritual Maturity**: Participating in spiritual practices together promotes spiritual maturity, as individuals and groups learn to embody Christ-like qualities and grow in their understanding of God's Word (2 Peter 3:18; Hebrews 5:12-14).

d. **Positive Influence**: Couples, families, and communities who engage in spiritual practices together serve as a positive influence on others, demonstrating the transformative power of faith and the importance of pursuing a relationship with God (Matthew 5:16; 1 Peter 2:12).

Conclusion

Growing together through spiritual practices is essential for deepening relationships with God and fostering unity among believers. By engaging in prayer, Bible study, worship, and service together, individuals, couples, families, and communities can experience the richness and fullness of a shared faith journey. Implementing practical steps, such as creating routines, establishing accountability, and being adaptable, can help ensure the ongoing success of these spiritual practices. The impact of growing together through spiritual practices includes strengthened faith, enhanced relationships, spiritual maturity, and a positive influence on others. Embracing the biblical call to engage in spiritual practices together enables believers to experience the joy, growth, and unity that God desires for His people.

3.5 The Power of Forgiveness and Reconciliation

Forgiveness and reconciliation are essential components of the Christian faith, reflecting the core message of God's love and grace through Jesus Christ. This comprehensive exploration will examine the biblical basis for forgiveness and reconciliation, drawing on conservative Christian interpretations.

1. **The Biblical Basis for Forgiveness and Reconciliation**

The Bible highlights the importance of forgiveness and reconciliation in our relationships with God and others:

a. **God's Forgiveness**: Scripture emphasizes that God, through Jesus Christ, forgives our sins, offering us redemption and eternal life (Ephesians 1:7; 1 John 1:9).

b. **Jesus' Teachings**: Jesus taught about the importance of forgiving others, even using parables to illustrate the power of forgiveness (Matthew 18:21-35; Luke 6:37).

c. **Reconciliation**: The Bible encourages believers to reconcile with one another, emphasizing that God desires peace and unity among His people (Matthew 5:23-24; 2 Corinthians 5:18-19).

2. **The Power of Forgiveness and Reconciliation**

Forgiveness and reconciliation have transformative effects on our lives:

a. **Personal Healing**: Forgiving others can lead to emotional and spiritual healing, as we release bitterness and resentment, and allow God's grace to renew our hearts (Ephesians 4:31-32; Colossians 3:13).

b. **Restored Relationships**: Reconciliation restores broken relationships, fostering trust, understanding, and renewed connections with others (Romans 12:18; 2 Corinthians 13:11).

c. **Spiritual Growth**: The process of forgiveness and reconciliation fosters spiritual growth, as we learn to embody Christlike qualities such as humility, compassion, and love (Colossians 3:12-14; Philippians 2:1-5).

3. Principles for Practicing Forgiveness and Reconciliation

To practice forgiveness and reconciliation, consider these biblical principles:

a. **Humility**: Approach others with a humble heart, recognizing our own shortcomings and need for forgiveness (Philippians 2:3-4; James 4:6).

b. **Empathy**: Seek to understand the other person's perspective, demonstrating empathy and compassion in our interactions (1 Peter 3:8; Romans 12:15).

c. **Genuine Repentance**: When seeking forgiveness, express sincere repentance for any wrongdoing, demonstrating a commitment to change (2 Corinthians 7:10; Acts 3:19).

d. **Grace**: Extend grace to others, recognizing that we have all received God's unmerited favor through Jesus Christ (Ephesians 2:8-9; Colossians 3:13).

4. Practical Steps for Forgiveness and Reconciliation

To implement forgiveness and reconciliation in our lives, consider these practical steps:

a. **Pray**: Seek God's guidance and strength in the process of forgiveness and reconciliation, asking Him to work in your heart and the hearts of others (Philippians 4:6-7; James 1:5).

b. **Communicate**: Openly and honestly discuss the issue, listening to one another's perspectives and expressing your thoughts and feelings with respect (Ephesians 4:25; James 1:19).

c. **Take Responsibility**: Accept responsibility for your part in the conflict, acknowledging any wrongdoing and seeking forgiveness (Matthew 7:3-5; 1 John 1:8-9).

d. **Work Together**: Collaborate with the other person to develop a plan for moving forward, establishing trust and fostering healing (Ecclesiastes 4:9-10; Romans 12:16).

Conclusion

The power of forgiveness and reconciliation is rooted in the Christian faith, embodying the love, grace, and mercy that God offers us through Jesus Christ. By embracing these principles, individuals can experience personal healing, restored relationships, and spiritual growth. Following the biblical teachings on forgiveness and reconciliation, we are called to practice humility, empathy, genuine repentance, and extend grace to others. By incorporating practical steps such as prayer, open communication, taking responsibility, and working together, we can navigate the challenges of forgiveness and reconciliation, ultimately reflecting the transformative power of God's love in our lives and relationships.

3.6 Supporting Each Other's Spiritual Growth

Supporting each other's spiritual growth is a key aspect of Christian relationships, as believers are called to encourage, uplift, and challenge one another in their walk with God. This comprehensive exploration will examine the biblical basis for supporting each other's spiritual growth, drawing on conservative Christian interpretations.

1. **The Biblical Basis for Supporting Each Other's Spiritual Growth**

The Bible emphasizes the importance of believers supporting one another in their spiritual journey:

a. **Encouragement**: Scripture instructs Christians to encourage one another in their faith, offering support and motivation (Hebrews 10:24-25; 1 Thessalonians 5:11).

b. **Accountability**: Believers are called to hold one another accountable, addressing sin and guiding each other in righteous living (Galatians 6:1-2; Proverbs 27:17).

c. **Teaching and Learning**: Christians are instructed to teach and learn from one another, growing in their understanding of God's Word (Colossians 3:16; 2 Timothy 2:2).

d. **Prayer**: Believers are encouraged to pray for one another, seeking God's guidance, protection, and blessing (James 5:16; Ephesians 6:18).

2. Principles for Supporting Each Other's Spiritual Growth

To support each other's spiritual growth, consider these biblical principles:

a. **Love**: Approach one another with genuine love and care, seeking the other person's well-being and spiritual growth (1 Corinthians 16:14; 1 Peter 4:8).

b. **Humility**: Cultivate humility in relationships, recognizing that we are all on a spiritual journey and can learn from one another (Philippians 2:3-4; 1 Peter 5:5).

c. **Patience**: Practice patience with one another, understanding that spiritual growth is a lifelong process (Ephesians 4:2; Colossians 3:12).

d. **Mutual Support**: Provide mutual support and encouragement, recognizing that we are all part of the body of Christ and need one another (1 Corinthians 12:25-26; Romans 12:5).

3. Practical Steps for Supporting Each Other's Spiritual Growth

To implement support for each other's spiritual growth, consider these practical steps:

a. **Share Your Journey**: Openly discuss your spiritual journey with others, including your struggles, victories, and insights (James 5:16; Proverbs 27:17).

b. **Study Together**: Engage in regular Bible study with fellow believers, seeking to deepen your understanding of God's Word (Acts 17:11; Hebrews 10:24-25).

c. **Pray Together**: Pray for and with one another, lifting up each other's needs and concerns before God (Matthew 18:19-20; Colossians 4:2).

d. **Serve Together**: Seek opportunities to serve together, using your unique gifts and abilities to further God's kingdom (1 Peter 4:10-11; Ephesians 4:15-16).

Conclusion

Supporting each other's spiritual growth is a vital aspect of Christian living, as believers are called to encourage, challenge, and uplift one another in their faith. By following biblical principles of love, humility, patience, and mutual support, Christians can foster spiritual growth within their relationships and communities. Engaging in practical steps such as sharing one's spiritual journey, studying the Bible together, praying together, and serving together can further enhance spiritual growth and unity among believers. As Christians strive to support one another's spiritual growth, they demonstrate the transformative power of Christ's love and the unity that God desires for His people.

Chapter 4: Finding Hope in Illness and Health Challenges

4.1 Trusting God's Plan for Your Health

Health is a vital aspect of our lives, and trusting in God's plan for our health is an important part of our Christian faith. This comprehensive exploration will examine the biblical basis for trusting God's plan for our health, drawing on conservative Christian interpretations.

1. **The Biblical Basis for Trusting God's Plan for Your Health**

The Bible provides guidance and encouragement for trusting in God's plan for our health:

a. **God as Creator**: Scripture reminds us that God is the Creator of our bodies and has intricately designed us (Psalm 139:13-14; Genesis 1:27).

b. **God as Healer**: The Bible portrays God as the Healer, capable of restoring health and providing comfort in times of illness (Exodus 15:26; Psalm 103:2-3).

c. **God's Sovereignty**: Scripture emphasizes God's sovereignty over all aspects of our lives, including our health (Proverbs 16:9; Matthew 10:29-31).

d. **Wisdom and Discernment**: The Bible encourages us to seek wisdom and discernment in making decisions related to our health (Proverbs 2:6-8; James 1:5).

2. **Principles for Trusting God's Plan for Your Health**

To trust in God's plan for our health, consider these biblical principles:

a. **Faith**: Trust in God's goodness and sovereignty, believing that He has our best interests at heart (Hebrews 11:1; Proverbs 3:5-6).

b. **Prayer**: Bring your health concerns and needs before God in prayer, asking for His guidance, healing, and strength (Philippians 4:6-7; James 5:13-16).

c. **Stewardship**: Recognize your responsibility to care for the body God has given you, making wise choices in areas such as diet, exercise, and rest (1 Corinthians 6:19-20; Romans 12:1).

d. **Community**: Seek support and encouragement from your Christian community, sharing your health journey with fellow believers (Galatians 6:2; 1 Thessalonians 5:11).

3. Practical Steps for Trusting God's Plan for Your Health

To implement trust in God's plan for your health, consider these practical steps:

a. **Educate Yourself**: Seek reliable information and resources to make informed decisions about your health (Proverbs 18:15; 2 Timothy 2:15).

b. **Consult Professionals**: Consult with healthcare professionals and seek their guidance on medical decisions and treatments (Proverbs 11:14; 15:22).

c. **Embrace a Balanced Lifestyle**: Strive to maintain a balanced lifestyle, including proper nutrition, regular exercise, and sufficient rest (1 Timothy 4:8; Psalm 127:2).

d. **Pray and Reflect**: Spend time in prayer and reflection, seeking God's guidance and wisdom in managing your health (Psalm 46:10; James 4:8).

Conclusion

Trusting in God's plan for our health involves recognizing His sovereignty, seeking His wisdom, and taking responsibility for our physical well-being. By embracing biblical principles such as faith, prayer, stewardship, and community, we can develop a greater trust in

God's plan for our health. Practical steps, such as educating ourselves, consulting professionals, embracing a balanced lifestyle, and engaging in prayer and reflection, can further strengthen our trust in God's plan for our health. As we trust in God's plan for our health, we can experience His peace and comfort, knowing that He is in control and working all things together for our good.

4.2 Seeking Strength and Peace an Accurate Understanding of God's Word

An accurate understanding of God's Word is crucial for our spiritual growth and well-being. It provides us with the strength and peace needed to navigate life's challenges and uncertainties. This comprehensive exploration will examine the biblical basis for seeking strength and peace through an accurate understanding of God's Word, drawing on conservative Christian interpretations.

1. **The Biblical Basis for Seeking Strength and Peace Through God's Word**

The Bible offers numerous insights into the importance of understanding God's Word for strength and peace:

a. **God's Word as Truth**: Scripture emphasizes that God's Word is the ultimate source of truth (John 17:17; 2 Timothy 3:16-17).

b. **Wisdom and Discernment**: The Bible encourages believers to seek wisdom and discernment by studying God's Word (Proverbs 2:6-8; James 1:5).

c. **Strength and Courage**: Scripture assures believers that God's Word provides strength and courage in times of need (Joshua 1:9; Isaiah 41:10).

d. **Peace and Assurance**: The Bible emphasizes that God's Word brings peace and assurance to those who trust in its promises (Philippians 4:6-7; John 14:27).

2. **Principles for Seeking Strength and Peace Through an Accurate Understanding of God's Word**

To seek strength and peace through an accurate understanding of God's Word, consider these biblical principles:

a. **Diligent Study**: Invest time and effort in studying the Bible, seeking to understand its teachings and apply them to your life (2 Timothy 2:15; Psalm 119:105).

b. **Prayerful Reflection**: Approach your study of Scripture with prayer, asking the Holy Spirit to guide your understanding and reveal God's truth to you (John 16:13; James 1:5).

c. **Humility**: Maintain a humble heart and be willing to learn from others, recognizing that we are all growing in our understanding of God's Word (Proverbs 1:7; James 3:13).

d. **Application**: Put God's Word into practice in your daily life, seeking to live in obedience to His commands (James 1:22; Matthew 7:24-27).

3. Practical Steps for Seeking Strength and Peace Through an Accurate Understanding of God's Word

To implement strength and peace through an accurate understanding of God's Word, consider these practical steps:

a. **Establish a Regular Routine**: Set aside regular time for Bible study and reflection, creating a habit of engaging with God's Word (Psalm 1:2; Acts 17:11).

b. **Utilize Resources**: Make use of Bible study resources, such as commentaries, dictionaries, and study guides, to deepen your understanding of Scripture (Proverbs 15:22; 1 Thessalonians 5:21).

c. **Join a Bible Study Group**: Participate in a Bible study group or engage in discussions with fellow believers to enhance your understanding and application of God's Word (Hebrews 10:24-25; Acts 2:42).

d. **Memorize Scripture**: Commit key verses and passages to memory, allowing God's Word to strengthen and encourage you in times of need (Psalm 119:11; Colossians 3:16).

Conclusion

Seeking strength and peace through an accurate understanding of God's Word is vital for our spiritual growth and well-being. By embracing biblical principles such as diligent study, prayerful reflection, humility, and application, we can deepen our understanding of Scripture and experience the strength and peace it provides. Practical steps, such as establishing a regular routine, utilizing resources, joining a Bible study group will get you there.

4.3 Nurturing Your Spiritual Health Amidst Illness

Nurturing your spiritual health amidst illness is an essential aspect of maintaining your faith and drawing closer to God during challenging times. This comprehensive exploration will examine the biblical basis for nurturing spiritual health amidst illness, drawing on conservative Christian interpretations.

1. **The Biblical Basis for Nurturing Spiritual Health Amidst Illness**

The Bible offers guidance and comfort for those facing illness, emphasizing the importance of maintaining spiritual health:

a. **God's Presence**: Scripture reassures believers of God's presence during times of illness, providing comfort and strength (Psalm 46:1-3; Isaiah 41:10).

b. **God's Sovereignty**: The Bible reminds us of God's sovereignty over all aspects of our lives, including our health and well-being (Job 42:2; Romans 8:28).

c. **Prayer**: Scripture encourages believers to turn to God in prayer during times of illness, seeking His healing, strength, and peace (Philippians 4:6-7; James 5:13-16).

d. **Hope**: The Bible offers hope amidst suffering, affirming the eternal promises of God and the ultimate healing found in Christ (2 Corinthians 4:16-18; Revelation 21:4).

2. Principles for Nurturing Spiritual Health Amidst Illness

To nurture spiritual health amidst illness, consider these biblical principles:

a. **Trust**: Place your trust in God's sovereignty and goodness, believing that He is with you during your illness and has a purpose for your suffering (Proverbs 3:5-6; Psalm 62:8).

b. **Prayer and Meditation**: Engage in regular prayer and meditation, seeking God's presence, guidance, and comfort (Psalm 62:5-8; Matthew 7:7-8).

c. **Scripture Reading**: Immerse yourself in God's Word, drawing strength, and hope from its promises and teachings (Psalm 119:50, 92; Romans 15:4).

d. **Community**: Lean on your Christian community for support, encouragement, and prayer during times of illness (Galatians 6:2; Hebrews 10:24-25).

3. Practical Steps for Nurturing Spiritual Health Amidst Illness

To nurture spiritual health amidst illness, consider these practical steps:

a. **Maintain a Prayer Routine**: Set aside regular time for prayer and reflection, inviting God's presence and comfort into your life (Psalm 55:17; Daniel 6:10).

b. **Read and Reflect on Scripture**: Read and meditate on passages that provide comfort, encouragement, and hope during times of illness (Psalm 23; Isaiah 40:28-31).

c. **Engage in Worship**: Participate in worship, either individually or with others, to remain connected to God and maintain a spirit of thankfulness (Psalm 95:1-7; Hebrews 12:28-29).

d. **Share Your Journey**: Open up to trusted friends, family members, or church members about your illness, allowing them to provide support, encouragement, and prayer (2 Corinthians 1:3-4; James 5:16).

Conclusion

Nurturing spiritual health amidst illness is essential for maintaining faith and drawing closer to God during challenging times. By embracing biblical principles such as trust, prayer and meditation, Scripture reading, and community, believers can nurture their spiritual health and experience God's comfort and strength. Implementing practical steps, such as maintaining a prayer routine, reading and reflecting on Scripture, engaging in worship, and sharing one's journey, can further strengthen spiritual health during times of illness.

4.4 Finding Purpose and Meaning in Your Suffering

Finding purpose and meaning in suffering is an essential aspect of the Christian faith, as it helps believers navigate trials and challenges with hope and resilience. This comprehensive exploration will examine the biblical basis for finding purpose and meaning in suffering, drawing on conservative Christian interpretations.

1. **The Biblical Basis for Finding Purpose and Meaning in Suffering**

The Bible offers insights into the purpose and meaning of suffering, providing believers with hope and perspective:

a. **Spiritual Growth**: Scripture teaches that suffering can lead to spiritual growth and maturity, refining our faith (James 1:2-4; Romans 5:3-5).

b. **God's Sovereignty**: The Bible emphasizes God's sovereignty over all circumstances, including suffering, and assures us that He can use suffering for our good and His glory (Romans 8:28; Genesis 50:20).

c. **Christ's Example**: Scripture reminds us of Jesus' own suffering and His ability to empathize with our struggles (Hebrews 4:15-16; 1 Peter 2:21).

d. **Eternal Perspective**: The Bible encourages us to maintain an eternal perspective, recognizing that our present suffering is temporary compared to the eternal glory we will experience in heaven (2 Corinthians 4:16-18; Romans 8:18).

2. Principles for Finding Purpose and Meaning in Suffering

To find purpose and meaning in suffering, consider these biblical principles:

a. **Trust**: Trust in God's sovereignty and goodness, believing that He has a purpose for your suffering and can bring good from it (Proverbs 3:5-6; Isaiah 55:8-9).

b. **Perseverance**: Endure suffering with perseverance, recognizing that it can produce character and hope (Romans 5:3-4; James 1:12).

c. **Prayer**: Turn to God in prayer during times of suffering, seeking His guidance, comfort, and strength (Psalm 34:17-18; Philippians 4:6-7).

d. **Community**: Lean on your Christian community for support, encouragement, and prayer during times of suffering (Galatians 6:2; 1 Thessalonians 5:11).

3. Practical Steps for Finding Purpose and Meaning in Suffering

To find purpose and meaning in suffering, consider these practical steps:

a. **Reflect on Scripture**: Meditate on biblical passages that address suffering, seeking wisdom and encouragement from God's Word (Psalm 119:50; Romans 8:18).

b. **Seek God's Purpose**: Pray for God to reveal His purpose in your suffering, asking Him to show you how He can use it for your growth and His glory (Jeremiah 29:11-13; Romans 8:28).

c. **Share Your Testimony**: Share your experience of suffering with others, offering hope and encouragement by testifying to God's faithfulness (2 Corinthians 1:3-4; 1 Peter 3:15).

d. **Serve Others**: Look for opportunities to serve and support others who are suffering, demonstrating God's love and compassion (Matthew 25:34-40; 1 Peter 4:10).

Conclusion

Finding purpose and meaning in suffering is a vital aspect of the Christian faith, as it helps believers navigate trials with hope and resilience. By embracing biblical principles such as trust, perseverance, prayer, and community, we can find purpose and meaning in our suffering. Implementing practical steps, such as reflecting on Scripture, seeking God's purpose, sharing our testimony, and serving others, can further strengthen our faith and understanding of suffering. As believers find purpose and meaning in their suffering, they will acquire the ability to remain faithful in difficult times.

4.5 Leaning on Your Faith Community for Support

Leaning on your faith community for support is an essential aspect of the Christian life, as it fosters unity, encouragement, and spiritual growth. This comprehensive exploration will examine the biblical basis for leaning on your faith community for support, drawing on conservative Christian interpretations.

1. **The Biblical Basis for Leaning on Your Faith Community for Support**

The Bible offers numerous insights into the importance of relying on your faith community for support:

a. **Unity in Christ**: Scripture emphasizes the unity of believers as members of the body of Christ, highlighting the interdependence of the community (1 Corinthians 12:12-27; Ephesians 4:15-16).

b. **Encouragement and Edification**: The Bible encourages believers to support, encourage, and edify one another within the faith community (1 Thessalonians 5:11; Hebrews 10:24-25).

c. **Bearing Burdens**: Scripture teaches that believers should bear each other's burdens, providing support and care during difficult times (Galatians 6:2; Romans 12:15).

d. **Spiritual Growth**: The Bible emphasizes the role of the faith community in promoting spiritual growth and maturity (Ephesians 4:11-14; Colossians 3:16).

2. Principles for Leaning on Your Faith Community for Support

To lean on your faith community for support, consider these biblical principles:

a. **Humility**: Approach your faith community with humility, recognizing your need for support and the interdependence of the body of Christ (Philippians 2:3-4; James 4:10).

b. **Vulnerability**: Be willing to share your struggles and needs with your faith community, allowing them to provide support and encouragement (James 5:16; 2 Corinthians 1:3-4).

c. **Active Participation**: Engage actively in the life of your faith community, attending worship services, small group gatherings, and other activities (Acts 2:42-47; Hebrews 10:24-25).

d. **Reciprocity**: Offer support and encouragement to others in your faith community, recognizing that we all need each other's support (1 Peter 4:10; 1 Corinthians 12:25-26).

3. Practical Steps for Leaning on Your Faith Community for Support

To lean on your faith community for support, consider these practical steps:

a. **Develop Relationships**: Cultivate meaningful relationships with fellow believers, investing time and effort in building connections within your faith community (Proverbs 17:17; 1 John 1:7).

b. **Seek Accountability**: Establish accountability relationships with trusted members of your faith community, providing mutual support and encouragement (Proverbs 27:17; Ecclesiastes 4:9-12).

c. **Participate in Small Groups**: Join a small group, Bible study, or prayer group within your faith community, allowing for deeper connections and opportunities for support (Acts 2:46-47; Colossians 3:16).

d. **Serve Together**: Engage in service opportunities alongside your faith community, building bonds of unity and support through shared experiences (Galatians 5:13; 1 Peter 4:10).

Conclusion

Leaning on your faith community for support is essential for fostering unity, encouragement, and spiritual growth. By embracing biblical principles such as humility, vulnerability, active participation, and reciprocity, believers can effectively lean on their faith community for support. Implementing practical steps, such as developing relationships, seeking accountability, participating in small groups, and serving together, can further strengthen bonds within the faith community. As believers lean on their faith community for support, they will have the strength to get through those difficult times.

4.6 Embracing God's Healing and Restoration

Embracing God's healing Word and the restoration He offers is essential for spiritual growth, renewal, and wholeness. This comprehensive exploration will examine the biblical basis for embracing God's healing Word and restoration, drawing on conservative Christian interpretations.

1. **The Biblical Basis for Embracing God's Healing Word and Restoration**

The Bible offers numerous insights into God's healing Word and the restoration He provides:

a. **God's Word as a Source of Healing**: Scripture reveals that God's Word has the power to bring healing and restoration to our lives (Psalm 107:20; Proverbs 4:20-22).

b. **God's Promises of Restoration**: The Bible is filled with promises of restoration for those who turn to God in repentance and faith (Joel 2:25-26; Isaiah 61:1-3).

c. **Jesus as the Healer**: Scripture portrays Jesus as the ultimate healer, both physically and spiritually, through His life, death, and resurrection (Matthew 8:16-17; 1 Peter 2:24).

d. **God's Restoration of Relationships**: The Bible emphasizes that God desires to restore relationships, both with Himself and with others (2 Corinthians 5:18-20; Matthew 5:23-24).

2. Principles for Embracing God's Healing Word and Restoration

To embrace God's healing Word and restoration, consider these biblical principles:

a. **Faith**: Trust in God's promises of healing and restoration, believing that He is faithful to fulfill His Word (Hebrews 11:1; Romans 4:20-21).

b. **Repentance**: Turn to God in repentance, acknowledging your need for His healing and restoration (Acts 3:19; 1 John 1:9).

c. **Prayer**: Seek God through prayer, asking for His healing and restoration in your life (James 5:16; Jeremiah 29:12-13).

d. **Obedience**: Obey God's Word, aligning your life with His will and allowing His healing and restoration to flow (John 15:7; 1 John 2:5).

3. Practical Steps for Embracing God's Healing Word and Restoration

To embrace God's healing Word and restoration, consider these practical steps:

a. **Meditate on Scripture**: Immerse yourself in God's Word, meditating on passages that reveal His promises of healing and restoration (Joshua 1:8; Psalm 119:15-16).

b. **Seek Forgiveness**: Confess your sins to God and seek forgiveness from those you have hurt, allowing for healing and restoration (James 5:16; Matthew 5:23-24).

c. **Pray for Healing and Restoration**: Pray regularly for God's healing and restoration in your life and the lives of others (James 5:13-16; Ephesians 6:18).

d. **Cultivate a Spirit of Gratitude**: Practice gratitude for God's healing and restoration in your life, acknowledging His goodness and faithfulness (1 Thessalonians 5:18; Psalm 9:1).

Conclusion

Embracing God's healing Word and restoration is essential for spiritual growth, renewal, and wholeness. By embracing biblical principles such as faith, repentance, prayer, and obedience, believers can experience God's healing Word and restoration. Implementing practical steps, such as meditating on Scripture, seeking forgiveness, praying for healing and restoration, and cultivating a spirit of gratitude, can further strengthen our relationship with God and embrace His healing and restorative work. As believers embrace God's healing Word and restoration, they will find the wisdom to get through those difficult times.

Chapter 5: Overcoming Joblessness and Financial Struggles

5.1 Trusting in God's Provision and Timing

Overcoming joblessness and financial struggles is a challenge many people face. As Christians, trusting in God's provision and timing is essential for navigating these difficulties with faith and hope. This comprehensive exploration will examine the biblical basis for overcoming joblessness and financial struggles, drawing on conservative Christian interpretations.

1. **The Biblical Basis for Trusting in God's Provision and Timing**

The Bible offers numerous insights into trusting in God's provision and timing during joblessness and financial struggles:

a. **God's Provision**: Scripture assures believers that God will provide for their needs (Matthew 6:25-34; Philippians 4:19).

b. **God's Timing**: The Bible teaches that God's timing is perfect, even when it may not align with our expectations (Ecclesiastes 3:1-8; Isaiah 55:8-9).

c. **God's Faithfulness**: Scripture emphasizes God's faithfulness and commitment to care for His people (Lamentations 3:22-23; Deuteronomy 31:6).

d. **God's Sovereignty**: The Bible highlights God's sovereignty over all aspects of life, including joblessness and financial struggles (Proverbs 16:9; Romans 8:28).

2. **Principles for Overcoming Joblessness and Financial Struggles**

To overcome joblessness and financial struggles, consider these biblical principles:

a. **Trust**: Trust in God's provision and timing, believing that He will meet your needs and guide you through difficult circumstances (Proverbs 3:5-6; 1 Peter 5:7).

b. **Contentment**: Cultivate a spirit of contentment, recognizing that true satisfaction comes from God rather than material wealth (Philippians 4:11-13; 1 Timothy 6:6-8).

c. **Stewardship**: Practice wise stewardship of your resources, seeking to honor God with your financial decisions (Proverbs 21:20; Matthew 25:14-30).

d. **Prayer**: Turn to God in prayer during joblessness and financial struggles, seeking His guidance, provision, and wisdom (James 1:5; Philippians 4:6-7).

3. Practical Steps for Overcoming Joblessness and Financial Struggles

To overcome joblessness and financial struggles, consider these practical steps:

a. **Seek Godly Counsel**: Consult with trusted Christian mentors, friends, or financial advisors who can offer biblical guidance and support (Proverbs 15:22; Proverbs 12:15).

b. **Create a Budget**: Develop a budget to manage your finances responsibly, prioritizing essential expenses and cutting back on non-essential items (Proverbs 27:23-24; Luke 14:28-30).

c. **Pursue Opportunities**: Actively seek job opportunities and explore potential career paths, trusting God's guidance and provision in the process (Proverbs 6:6-11; Colossians 3:23-24).

d. **Serve Others**: Look for ways to serve others, even during times of joblessness and financial struggles, as this can bring joy and purpose to your life (Galatians 6:9-10; Acts 20:35).

Conclusion

Overcoming joblessness and financial struggles involves trusting in God's provision and timing, as well as embracing biblical principles such as trust, contentment, stewardship, and prayer. By implementing practical steps, such as seeking godly counsel, creating a budget, pursuing opportunities, and serving others, believers can navigate these challenges with faith and hope. As Christians trust in God's provision and timing, they can experience His peace and endure the difficult times that lie ahead.

5.2 Cultivating a Heart of Contentment

Overcoming joblessness and financial struggles can be challenging, but cultivating a heart of contentment can help us navigate these difficulties with a sense of peace and trust in God. This comprehensive exploration will examine the biblical basis for cultivating contentment during joblessness and financial struggles, drawing on conservative Christian interpretations.

1. **The Biblical Basis for Cultivating a Heart of Contentment**

The Bible offers numerous insights into cultivating a heart of contentment during joblessness and financial struggles:

a. **God's Provision**: Scripture reminds us that our ultimate source of provision and security is God, not our jobs or material possessions (Matthew 6:25-34; Philippians 4:19).

b. **The Danger of Materialism**: The Bible warns against the dangers of materialism and the pursuit of wealth, as they can lead to discontentment and misplaced priorities (1 Timothy 6:6-10; Luke 12:15).

c. **The Value of Contentment**: Scripture highlights the importance of contentment, describing it as a source of great gain and peace (Hebrews 13:5; Proverbs 15:16).

d. **The Example of Christ**: Jesus' life exemplifies contentment, as He chose to focus on God's will and serving others rather than pursuing material wealth (Matthew 8:20; 2 Corinthians 8:9).

2. **Principles for Cultivating a Heart of Contentment**

To cultivate a heart of contentment during joblessness and financial struggles, consider these biblical principles:

a. **Trust in God**: Rely on God's faithfulness and provision, trusting that He will meet your needs according to His perfect plan (Proverbs 3:5-6; 1 Peter 5:7).

b. **Focus on Eternal Priorities**: Keep your focus on eternal priorities, such as your relationship with God and the well-being of others, rather than material possessions (Matthew 6:19-21; Colossians 3:1-2).

c. **Practice Gratitude**: Cultivate an attitude of gratitude, acknowledging the blessings God has provided and recognizing His faithfulness (1 Thessalonians 5:18; Psalm 136).

d. **Embrace Simplicity**: Choose to live a life of simplicity, valuing relationships and experiences over material possessions (Proverbs 30:8-9; Luke 12:22-34).

3. Practical Steps for Cultivating a Heart of Contentment

To cultivate a heart of contentment during joblessness and financial struggles, consider these practical steps:

a. **Daily Devotion**: Spend time in prayer and Bible study each day, allowing God's Word to shape your perspective and priorities (Psalm 1:1-3; Colossians 3:16).

b. **Count Your Blessings**: Regularly reflect on the blessings in your life, focusing on the positive aspects rather than dwelling on difficulties (Psalm 103:1-5; Philippians 4:8).

c. **Practice Generosity**: Look for opportunities to give to others, even in times of financial struggle, as this can foster a heart of contentment (Proverbs 11:24-25; 2 Corinthians 9:6-8).

d. **Seek Support**: Reach out to friends, family, and your faith community for encouragement and support during difficult times (Galatians 6:2; Ecclesiastes 4:9-12).

Conclusion

Cultivating a heart of contentment during joblessness and financial struggles is essential for maintaining spiritual well-being and trust in God. By embracing biblical principles such as trust in God, focusing on eternal priorities in God, practicing gratitude, and embracing simplicity, believers can nurture a heart of contentment amidst life's challenges. Implementing practical steps, such as daily devotion, counting your blessings, practicing generosity, and seeking support from others, can further strengthen your ability to cultivate contentment during joblessness and financial struggles.

By focusing on our relationship with God and the blessings He provides, believers can overcome the challenges of joblessness and financial struggles while maintaining a heart of contentment. This contentment will lead to greater spiritual growth, resilience, and a deeper sense of God's presence and provision in our lives.

5.3 Seeking God's Wisdom for Financial Stewardship

Overcoming joblessness and financial struggles is a challenge many people face. As Christians, seeking God's wisdom for financial stewardship is crucial for navigating these difficulties while honoring Him with our resources. This comprehensive exploration will examine the biblical basis for seeking God's wisdom for financial stewardship during joblessness and financial struggles, drawing on conservative Christian interpretations.

1. The Biblical Basis for Seeking God's Wisdom for Financial Stewardship

The Bible offers numerous insights into seeking God's wisdom for financial stewardship during joblessness and financial struggles:

a. **God's Ownership**: Scripture teaches that God is the ultimate owner of everything, and we are stewards of the resources He entrusts to us (Psalm 24:1; 1 Chronicles 29:11-12).

b. **Wisdom and Discernment**: The Bible emphasizes the importance of seeking wisdom and discernment in all aspects of life, including financial matters (Proverbs 2:1-7; James 1:5).

c. **Stewardship Principles**: Scripture provides guidelines and principles for managing our resources responsibly (Proverbs 3:9-10; Luke 16:10-12).

d. **God's Blessing and Provision**: The Bible assures believers that God will provide for their needs and bless those who are faithful stewards (Matthew 6:25-34; Malachi 3:10).

2. Principles for Seeking God's Wisdom for Financial Stewardship

To seek God's wisdom for financial stewardship during joblessness and financial struggles, consider these biblical principles:

a. **Prayer and Dependence on God**: Turn to God in prayer, seeking His guidance and wisdom in your financial decisions (Philippians 4:6-7; Jeremiah 33:3).

b. **Honoring God with Your Resources**: Prioritize honoring God with your resources, including tithes and offerings, even during financial struggles (Proverbs 3:9-10; 2 Corinthians 9:6-7).

c. **Living Within Your Means**: Strive to live within your means, avoiding debt and exercising self-control in your spending habits (Proverbs 22:7; Romans 13:8).

d. **Planning and Saving**: Practice wise planning and saving to prepare for future needs and emergencies (Proverbs 6:6-8; Proverbs 21:20).

3. Practical Steps for Seeking God's Wisdom for Financial Stewardship

To seek God's wisdom for financial stewardship during joblessness and financial struggles, consider these practical steps:

a. **Develop a Budget**: Create a budget that reflects your current financial situation and prioritizes essential expenses, while seeking God's guidance (Luke 14:28-30; Proverbs 27:23-24).

b. **Seek Godly Counsel**: Consult with trusted Christian mentors, friends, or financial advisors who can offer biblical guidance and support (Proverbs 15:22; Proverbs 19:20).

c. **Reduce Expenses**: Look for ways to reduce expenses and eliminate non-essential spending, allowing you to better steward your resources (Proverbs 21:20; Ecclesiastes 5:10).

d. **Pursue Income Opportunities**: Actively seek job opportunities and explore potential career paths, trusting in God's provision and guidance (Proverbs 16:3; Colossians 3:23-24).

Conclusion

Seeking God's wisdom for financial stewardship during joblessness and financial struggles involves embracing biblical principles and implementing practical steps. By turning to God in prayer, honoring Him with our resources, living within our means, and planning and saving, we can better navigate these challenges while strengthening our faith and trust in God's provision. Developing a budget, seeking godly counsel, reducing expenses, and pursuing income opportunities are practical steps that can help us manage our financial resources responsibly during difficult times.

By relying on God's wisdom and guidance, we can overcome joblessness and financial struggles with a sense of peace and confidence in His plan for our lives. This approach will not only help us manage our resources more effectively but will also deepen our relationship with God and cultivate a heart of contentment and gratitude, even in the midst of adversity.

5.4 Harnessing the Power of Prayer in Job Hunting

Overcoming joblessness and financial struggles can be a daunting challenge for many individuals. As Christians, harnessing the power of prayer in job hunting is a crucial aspect of navigating this difficult time while maintaining trust in God's provision and guidance. This comprehensive exploration will examine the biblical basis for harnessing the power of prayer in job hunting, drawing on conservative Christian interpretations.

1. The Biblical Basis for Harnessing the Power of Prayer in Job Hunting

The Bible underscores the importance of prayer as a means of seeking God's guidance, wisdom, and provision in all aspects of life, including job hunting:

a. **Prayer and Dependence on God**: Scripture encourages believers to turn to God in prayer for guidance and help in times of need (Philippians 4:6-7; 1 Peter 5:7).

b. **God's Provision**: The Bible assures us that God will provide for our needs, even in times of joblessness and financial struggles (Matthew 6:25-34; Psalm 34:10).

c. **Seeking God's Will**: Scripture emphasizes the importance of seeking God's will in all areas of life, including our careers (Proverbs 3:5-6; Romans 12:2).

2. Principles for Harnessing the Power of Prayer in Job Hunting

To harness the power of prayer in job hunting during joblessness and financial struggles, consider these biblical principles:

a. **Pray Specifically**: Be specific in your prayers, asking God for guidance, opportunities, and wisdom in your job search (Matthew 7:7-8; James 1:5).

b. **Pray Persistently**: Remain persistent in your prayers, trusting in God's timing and provision (Luke 18:1-8; 1 Thessalonians 5:17).

c. **Pray with Faith**: Approach your prayers with faith, believing that God hears you and will provide according to His perfect will (Mark 11:24; Hebrews 11:6).

d. **Pray with Thanksgiving**: Express gratitude in your prayers, acknowledging God's goodness and provision in your life (Philippians 4:6; 1 Thessalonians 5:18).

3. Practical Steps for Harnessing the Power of Prayer in Job Hunting

To harness the power of prayer in job hunting during joblessness and financial struggles, consider these practical steps:

a. **Create a Prayer Routine**: Set aside time each day to pray specifically for your job search, asking for God's guidance and provision (Psalm 5:3; Daniel 6:10).

b. **Pray for Others**: Pray for others who are also experiencing joblessness and financial struggles, asking God to provide for their needs as well (James 5:16; 1 Timothy 2:1).

c. **Seek Support in Prayer**: Share your prayer requests with fellow believers, asking them to pray with you and for you in your job search (Matthew 18:19-20; Ephesians 6:18).

d. **Reflect on God's Word**: Meditate on Scripture passages that offer encouragement and guidance during your job search, applying them to your specific situation (Joshua 1:8; Psalm 119:105).

Conclusion

Harnessing the power of prayer in job hunting during joblessness and financial struggles involves embracing biblical principles and implementing practical steps. By praying specifically, persistently, with faith and thanksgiving, believers can navigate the challenges of joblessness while maintaining trust in God's guidance and provision. Creating a prayer routine, praying for others, seeking support in prayer, and reflecting on God's Word can further strengthen our faith.

5.5 Building Resilience Through Faith and Perseverance

Overcoming joblessness and financial struggles requires resilience, a quality that can be nurtured through faith and perseverance. As Christians, turning to biblical principles can help us build resilience during challenging times. This comprehensive exploration will examine the biblical basis for building resilience through faith and perseverance, drawing on conservative Christian interpretations.

1. The Biblical Basis for Building Resilience Through Faith and Perseverance

The Bible provides numerous examples and teachings on the importance of faith and perseverance in overcoming difficulties, including joblessness and financial struggles:

a. **Perseverance in Trials**: Scripture encourages believers to persevere in the face of trials, recognizing that such experiences can develop our character and deepen our faith (James 1:2-4; Romans 5:3-5).

b. **Faith in God's Provision**: The Bible teaches that faith in God's provision and promises can help us navigate challenging times (Hebrews 11:1; Matthew 6:25-34).

c. **Strength in Weakness**: Scripture reminds us that God's strength is made perfect in our weakness, and that we can find solace in Him during difficult times (2 Corinthians 12:9-10; Isaiah 40:29-31).

2. Principles for Building Resilience Through Faith and Perseverance

To build resilience through faith and perseverance during joblessness and financial struggles, consider these biblical principles:

a. **Trust in God**: Cultivate a deep trust in God's sovereignty, believing that He is in control of all circumstances and that He will provide for your needs (Proverbs 3:5-6; Psalm 37:3-6).

b. **Embrace Growth**: View challenging times as opportunities for growth and refinement of your character, faith, and relationship with God (James 1:2-4; 1 Peter 1:6-7).

c. **Maintain a Long-term Perspective**: Focus on the eternal perspective rather than temporary circumstances, recognizing that present struggles can yield spiritual fruit and eternal rewards (2 Corinthians 4:16-18; Colossians 3:2).

3. Practical Steps for Building Resilience Through Faith and Perseverance

To build resilience through faith and perseverance during joblessness and financial struggles, consider these practical steps:

a. **Cultivate a Daily Relationship with God**: Spend time in prayer and Bible study each day, seeking God's guidance, wisdom, and strength (Psalm 1:1-3; Matthew 6:33).

b. **Surround Yourself with Support**: Seek fellowship with other believers who can offer encouragement, prayer, and accountability during challenging times (Hebrews 10:24-25; Ecclesiastes 4:9-12).

c. **Practice Gratitude**: Develop a habit of expressing gratitude for God's provision, even in the midst of difficulties (1 Thessalonians 5:18; Philippians 4:6).

d. **Serve Others**: Focus on serving others, using your gifts and talents to bless others, which can provide a sense of purpose and meaning during joblessness and financial struggles (Galatians 6:9-10; 1 Peter 4:10).

Conclusion

Building resilience through faith and perseverance during joblessness and financial struggles involves embracing biblical principles and implementing practical steps. By trusting in God, embracing growth, and maintaining a long-term perspective, we can navigate these challenges with confidence, knowing that God is at work in our lives, even during difficult times. Cultivating a daily relationship with God, surrounding ourselves with support, practicing gratitude, and serving others can further strengthen our resilience, enabling us to cope with the difficult times in Satan's world.

5.6 Embracing New Opportunities with God's Guidance

In times of joblessness and financial struggles, it is essential to embrace new opportunities with God's guidance. As Christians, we are called to trust in God's plan and follow His leading, even when faced with uncertainty. This comprehensive exploration will examine the biblical basis for embracing new opportunities with God's guidance, drawing on conservative Christian interpretations.

1. The Biblical Basis for Embracing New Opportunities with God's Guidance

The Bible offers numerous teachings and examples illustrating the importance of embracing new opportunities with God's guidance during times of uncertainty:

a. **God's Plan**: Scripture emphasizes that God has a plan and purpose for our lives, even when we face joblessness and financial struggles (Jeremiah 29:11; Proverbs 16:9).

b. **God's Guidance**: The Bible underscores the importance of seeking God's guidance when making decisions and embracing new opportunities (Proverbs 3:5-6; James 1:5).

c. **Trust in God's Provision**: Scripture encourages us to trust in God's provision, even when facing challenges (Matthew 6:25-34; Philippians 4:19).

2. Principles for Embracing New Opportunities with God's Guidance

To embrace new opportunities with God's guidance during joblessness and financial struggles, consider these biblical principles:

a. **Pray for Wisdom**: Seek God's wisdom through prayer, asking for clarity and discernment as you explore new opportunities (James 1:5; Colossians 1:9).

b. **Be Open to God's Leading**: Be receptive to God's leading, even if it means stepping out of your comfort zone or pursuing an unexpected path (Isaiah 30:21; Psalm 37:23).

c. **Remain Faithful**: Trust in God's faithfulness, believing that He will provide for your needs and guide you through the challenges you face (Deuteronomy 31:6; Hebrews 10:23).

3. Practical Steps for Embracing New Opportunities with God's Guidance

To embrace new opportunities with God's guidance during joblessness and financial struggles, consider these practical steps:

a. **Reflect on Your Skills and Passions**: Assess your skills, interests, and passions, and explore how they might align with new opportunities (Romans 12:6-8; 1 Peter 4:10).

b. **Seek Wise Counsel**: Consult with trusted Christian friends, mentors, or spiritual leaders for advice and insight as you consider new opportunities (Proverbs 11:14; Proverbs 15:22).

c. **Research and Prepare**: Thoroughly research potential opportunities and prepare yourself by acquiring necessary skills or knowledge (Proverbs 24:27; 2 Timothy 2:15).

d. **Trust God's Timing**: Be patient and trust in God's timing, recognizing that He may open doors at the right time according to His plan (Ecclesiastes 3:1; Galatians 6:9).

Conclusion

Embracing new opportunities with God's guidance during joblessness and financial struggles involves drawing on biblical principles and implementing practical steps. By praying for wisdom, being open to God's leading, and remaining faithful, we can navigate these challenges with confidence, knowing that God will provide and guide us. Reflecting on our skills and passions, seeking wise counsel, researching and preparing, and trusting in God's timing can further help us to embrace new opportunities as we trust in God's plan for our lives.

Chapter 6: Alleviating Daily Stress with God's Help

6.1 Developing a God-Centered Perspective on Stress

Alleviating daily stress with God's help involves developing a God-centered perspective on stress, which can help us better manage the challenges we face. This comprehensive exploration will examine the biblical basis for developing a God-centered perspective on stress, drawing on conservative Christian interpretations.

1. **The Biblical Basis for Developing a God-Centered Perspective on Stress**

The Bible provides several teachings and insights that can help us develop a God-centered perspective on stress:

a. **God's Presence**: Scripture emphasizes that God is with us and will never leave us, even during times of stress (Deuteronomy 31:6; Psalm 46:1).

b. **Casting Our Cares**: The Bible instructs us to cast our cares and anxieties on God, knowing that He cares for us (1 Peter 5:7; Philippians 4:6-7).

c. **Seeking God's Peace**: Scripture points to the importance of seeking God's peace, which transcends understanding and guards our hearts and minds (Philippians 4:6-7; John 14:27).

2. **Principles for Developing a God-Centered Perspective on Stress**

To develop a God-centered perspective on stress, consider these biblical principles:

a. **Trust in God's Sovereignty**: Recognize that God is in control of all circumstances, and trust in His sovereignty over our lives (Proverbs 3:5-6; Isaiah 41:10).

b. **Focus on Eternal Priorities**: Keep your focus on eternal priorities rather than temporary, worldly concerns (Colossians 3:2; Matthew 6:33).

c. **Practice Gratitude**: Cultivate an attitude of gratitude, thanking God for His blessings and provision, even in the midst of stress (1 Thessalonians 5:18; Psalm 118:24).

3. Practical Steps for Developing a God-Centered Perspective on Stress

To develop a God-centered perspective on stress, consider these practical steps:

a. **Daily Time with God**: Spend time in prayer and Bible study each day, seeking God's guidance, wisdom, and strength (Psalm 1:1-3; Matthew 6:33).

b. **Surrender Control**: Release the need to control every aspect of your life and surrender your concerns and worries to God (Proverbs 3:5-6; Psalm 55:22).

c. **Mindfulness and Meditation**: Practice mindfulness and meditate on God's Word, allowing it to shape your thoughts and responses to stress (Psalm 119:15; Joshua 1:8).

d. **Seek Support**: Surround yourself with a supportive Christian community that can provide encouragement, prayer, and accountability during times of stress (Hebrews 10:24-25; Ecclesiastes 4:9-12).

Conclusion

Developing a God-centered perspective on stress involves embracing biblical principles and implementing practical steps. By trusting in God's sovereignty, focusing on eternal priorities, and practicing gratitude, we can better manage daily stress with God's help. Spending time with God, surrendering control, practicing mindfulness and meditation, and seeking support from a Christian community can further help us alleviate stress and maintain a God-centered perspective.

6.2 Prioritizing Prayer and Meditation in Daily Life

Alleviating daily stress with God's help requires prioritizing prayer and meditation in our daily lives. This comprehensive exploration will examine the biblical basis for prioritizing prayer and meditation and how they can help us manage stress, drawing on conservative Christian interpretations.

1. The Biblical Basis for Prioritizing Prayer and Meditation in Daily Life

The Bible emphasizes the importance of prayer and meditation in our daily lives to help us manage stress:

a. **Prayer**: Scripture encourages us to pray without ceasing and to present our requests to God, knowing that He hears and answers our prayers (1 Thessalonians 5:17; Philippians 4:6-7).

b. **Meditation**: The Bible highlights the value of meditating on God's Word, allowing it to shape our thoughts, actions, and responses to stress (Psalm 1:1-3; Joshua 1:8).

2. Principles for Prioritizing Prayer and Meditation in Daily Life

To prioritize prayer and meditation in daily life, consider these biblical principles:

a. **Consistency**: Develop a consistent prayer and meditation routine, setting aside regular time to connect with God (Mark 1:35; Psalm 63:1).

b. **Honesty**: Approach God with honesty and openness, expressing your emotions, worries, and concerns in prayer (Psalm 62:8; Hebrews 4:16).

c. **Focus on God's Attributes**: Meditate on the attributes of God, such as His love, faithfulness, and sovereignty, to deepen your trust in Him during times of stress (Psalm 145:8-9; Lamentations 3:22-23).

3. Practical Steps for Prioritizing Prayer and Meditation in Daily Life

To prioritize prayer and meditation in daily life, consider these practical steps:

a. **Designate a Specific Time and Place**: Create a designated time and place for daily prayer and meditation, making it a priority in your routine (Daniel 6:10; Luke 5:16).

b. **Use a Prayer Journal**: Keep a prayer journal to record your prayers, reflections, and insights from your time with God (Habakkuk 2:2; Psalm 102:18).

c. **Memorize Scripture**: Memorize key Bible verses that provide comfort, encouragement, and guidance during times of stress (Psalm 119:11; Colossians 3:16).

d. **Incorporate Silence and Listening**: Include periods of silence and active listening during your prayer and meditation time, allowing God to speak to you (1 Kings 19:11-13; Psalm 46:10).

Conclusion

Prioritizing prayer and meditation in daily life is essential for alleviating stress with God's help. By following biblical principles and implementing practical steps, we can create a consistent routine that deepens our relationship with God and helps us manage stress. Embracing honesty, focusing on God's attributes, designating a specific time and place, using a prayer journal, memorizing scripture, and incorporating silence and listening all contribute to a fruitful and stress-reducing prayer and meditation practice.

6.3 Learning to Surrender Control to God

One key aspect of alleviating daily stress with God's help is learning to surrender control to Him. This comprehensive exploration will examine the biblical basis for surrendering control to God and how doing so can help us manage stress, drawing on conservative Christian interpretations.

1. The Biblical Basis for Surrendering Control to God

The Bible provides several teachings and insights on the importance of surrendering control to God:

a. **Trust in God**: Scripture encourages us to trust in God's sovereignty and wisdom rather than relying solely on our own understanding (Proverbs 3:5-6; Isaiah 55:8-9).

b. **God's Strength in Weakness**: The Bible teaches that God's strength is made perfect in our weakness, and when we surrender our control, we can experience His power at work in our lives (2 Corinthians 12:9-10; Philippians 4:13).

c. **Cast Your Cares**: The Bible instructs us to cast our burdens upon God, knowing that He cares for us and will sustain us (Psalm 55:22; 1 Peter 5:7).

2. Principles for Surrendering Control to God

To surrender control to God, consider these biblical principles:

a. **Acknowledge Your Limitations**: Recognize that you are not in control of every aspect of your life and that you need God's help (Jeremiah 10:23; Isaiah 40:28-31).

b. **Dependence on God**: Cultivate a heart of dependence on God, seeking His guidance, wisdom, and provision in all aspects of life (John 15:5; Psalm 121:1-2).

c. **Obedience**: Submit to God's will and obey His commands, trusting that He knows what is best for you (James 4:7-8; Psalm 143:10).

3. Practical Steps for Surrendering Control to God

To surrender control to God, consider these practical steps:

a. **Daily Prayer**: Make prayer a daily priority, inviting God into every aspect of your life and asking for His guidance (Philippians 4:6-7; 1 Thessalonians 5:17).

b. **Release Worry**: Let go of worry and anxiety by consciously choosing to trust in God's promises and His ability to care for you (Matthew 6:25-34; Philippians 4:6-7).

c. **Embrace Flexibility**: Practice flexibility and adaptability, allowing God to direct your path and being open to change (James 4:13-15; Proverbs 16:9).

d. **Seek Godly Counsel**: Seek wisdom and guidance from mature Christians and biblical teachings to help you discern God's direction (Proverbs 15:22; Proverbs 11:14).

Conclusion

Learning to surrender control to God is an essential aspect of alleviating daily stress with His help. By embracing biblical principles and implementing practical steps, we can relinquish control and experience greater peace and trust in God's guidance. Acknowledging our limitations, cultivating dependence on God, practicing obedience, praying daily, releasing worry, embracing flexibility, and seeking godly counsel are all vital components of surrendering control and managing stress with God's help.

6.4 Implementing God's Wisdom in Time Management

Effective time management is essential for alleviating daily stress with God's help. This comprehensive exploration will examine the biblical basis for implementing God's wisdom in time management and how it can help us manage stress, drawing on conservative Christian interpretations.

1. **The Biblical Basis for Implementing God's Wisdom in Time Management**

The Bible provides guidance and insights on the importance of time management and using God's wisdom to navigate our daily schedules:

a. **Redeeming the Time**: Scripture encourages us to make the most of our time, recognizing that our days are numbered (Ephesians 5:15-16; Psalm 90:12).

b. **Prioritizing God's Kingdom**: The Bible teaches that we should prioritize seeking God's kingdom above all else, trusting that our other needs will be met (Matthew 6:33; Colossians 3:1-2).

c. **Rest and Sabbath**: God's Word highlights the importance of rest and maintaining a healthy work-life balance (Genesis 2:2-3; Exodus 20:8-11).

2. Principles for Implementing God's Wisdom in Time Management

To implement God's wisdom in time management, consider these biblical principles:

a. **Discernment**: Develop discernment in distinguishing between essential and non-essential tasks, prioritizing what is truly important (Philippians 1:9-10; Proverbs 3:21-26).

b. **Stewardship**: Recognize that time is a gift from God and strive to be a good steward of the time you have been given (Colossians 4:5; 1 Peter 4:10).

c. **Balance**: Seek balance in all aspects of life, including work, rest, and spiritual growth (Ecclesiastes 3:1-8; Luke 10:38-42).

3. Practical Steps for Implementing God's Wisdom in Time Management

To implement God's wisdom in time management, consider these practical steps:

a. **Plan and Organize**: Create a daily, weekly, and monthly schedule that reflects your priorities and includes time for work, rest, and spiritual growth (Proverbs 21:5; Luke 14:28).

b. **Set Realistic Goals**: Establish attainable goals for various aspects of your life, allowing room for flexibility and adjustments (Proverbs 16:9; James 4:13-15).

c. **Delegate and Collaborate**: Share responsibilities and tasks with others when appropriate, recognizing the value of teamwork and cooperation (Exodus 18:13-27; 1 Corinthians 12:12-27).

d. **Regularly Evaluate**: Periodically assess your time management and priorities, making adjustments as needed to maintain a balanced and God-honoring lifestyle (2 Corinthians 13:5; Lamentations 3:40).

Conclusion

Implementing God's wisdom in time management is crucial for alleviating daily stress with His help. By following biblical principles and practical steps, we can make the most of our time and live a balanced and purposeful life. Embracing discernment, stewardship, and balance, along with planning and organizing, setting realistic goals, delegating and collaborating, and regularly evaluating our priorities, are all essential components of time management that can reduce stress and promote spiritual growth.

6.5 Cultivating a Spirit of Joy and Peace

Cultivating a spirit of joy and peace is essential for alleviating daily stress with God's help. This comprehensive exploration will examine the biblical basis for nurturing joy and peace in our lives and how it can help us manage stress, drawing on conservative Christian interpretations.

1. The Biblical Basis for Cultivating Joy and Peace

The Bible provides several teachings and insights on the importance of joy and peace in our lives:

a. **The Fruit of the Spirit**: Joy and peace are listed among the fruit of the Spirit, which are attributes that characterize a life led by the Holy Spirit (Galatians 5:22-23; Romans 14:17).

b. **Rejoicing in the Lord**: Scripture encourages us to find our joy in the Lord, recognizing that He is the source of our true happiness (Philippians 4:4; Psalm 16:11).

c. **God's Peace**: The Bible teaches that we can experience God's peace, which surpasses all understanding, when we trust in Him and submit our anxieties to Him (Philippians 4:6-7; John 14:27).

2. **Principles for Cultivating Joy and Peace**

To cultivate joy and peace in our lives, consider these biblical principles:

a. **Focus on God**: Keep your focus on God and His goodness, recognizing that He is the source of joy and peace (Hebrews 12:2; Isaiah 26:3).

b. **Gratitude**: Cultivate a heart of gratitude by regularly thanking God for His blessings and provision (1 Thessalonians 5:16-18; Colossians 3:15-17).

c. **Trust in God**: Trust in God's sovereignty and love, believing that He is working all things for your good (Romans 8:28; Proverbs 3:5-6).

3. **Practical Steps for Cultivating Joy and Peace**

To cultivate joy and peace, consider these practical steps:

a. **Daily Prayer and Meditation**: Spend time daily in prayer and meditation, seeking God's presence and guidance (Psalm 46:10; Matthew 6:6).

b. **Worship and Praise**: Engage in regular worship and praise, expressing your love and adoration for God (Psalm 100:1-5; Ephesians 5:18-20).

c. **Scripture Reading**: Read and meditate on Scripture, allowing God's Word to shape your thoughts and attitudes (Joshua 1:8; Psalm 119:105).

d. **Fellowship**: Build and maintain relationships with other believers, encouraging one another in your walk with God (Hebrews 10:24-25; Acts 2:42-47).

Conclusion

Cultivating a spirit of joy and peace is vital for alleviating daily stress with God's help. By embracing biblical principles and implementing practical steps, we can nurture joy and peace in our lives, allowing us to better manage stress and maintain a close relationship with God. Focusing on God, cultivating gratitude, trusting in His sovereignty, engaging in daily prayer and meditation, worshiping and praising, reading Scripture, and nurturing fellowship with other believers are all essential components of nurturing a spirit of joy and peace, leading to a more fulfilling and stress-free life.

6.6 Strengthening Your Faith Through Life's Challenges

Strengthening your faith through life's challenges is an essential aspect of alleviating daily stress with God's help. This comprehensive exploration will examine the biblical basis for fortifying your faith amidst difficulties and how it can help manage stress, drawing on conservative Christian interpretations.

1. The Biblical Basis for Strengthening Faith in Challenges

The Bible provides numerous examples and teachings on the importance of strengthening faith during life's challenges:

a. **Tested Faith**: The Bible teaches that trials and difficulties serve to test and refine our faith, producing steadfastness and maturity (James 1:2-4; 1 Peter 1:6-7).

b. **God's Presence**: Scripture reassures us that God is with us during our struggles and that He will provide the strength and comfort we need (Isaiah 41:10; 2 Corinthians 1:3-4).

c. **Trust in God**: The Bible encourages us to trust in God's sovereignty and His good plan for our lives, even during times of hardship (Proverbs 3:5-6; Romans 8:28).

2. Principles for Strengthening Faith in Challenges

To strengthen your faith during life's challenges, consider these biblical principles:

a. **Prayer**: Maintain an open line of communication with God through prayer, expressing your needs and concerns while also listening for His guidance (Philippians 4:6-7; 1 Thessalonians 5:17).

b. **Scripture Study**: Regularly study Scripture to gain wisdom and encouragement from God's Word (Psalm 119:105; 2 Timothy 3:16-17).

c. **Dependence on God**: Acknowledge your need for God's help and rely on His strength instead of your own (2 Corinthians 12:9-10; Psalm 46:1-3).

d. **Perseverance**: Remain steadfast in your faith and continue to trust God, even when circumstances are difficult (Hebrews 12:1-2; James 1:12).

3. Practical Steps for Strengthening Faith in Challenges

To strengthen your faith amidst challenges, consider these practical steps:

a. **Cultivate a Strong Prayer Life**: Dedicate time daily to prayer, seeking God's presence and guidance (Matthew 6:6; Luke 18:1).

b. **Engage in Regular Scripture Reading**: Immerse yourself in the Bible to grow in your understanding of God's promises and character (Joshua 1:8; Colossians 3:16).

c. **Fellowship**: Surround yourself with other believers who can encourage, support, and pray for you during life's challenges (Hebrews 10:24-25; Ecclesiastes 4:9-12).

d. **Serve Others**: Find opportunities to serve others in your church and community, which can help shift your focus from your own struggles and foster spiritual growth (Galatians 5:13-14; 1 Peter 4:10).

Conclusion

Strengthening your faith through life's challenges is crucial for alleviating daily stress with God's help. By embracing biblical principles and implementing practical steps, we can fortify our faith amidst difficulties, allowing us to better manage stress and maintain a close relationship with God. Prayer, Scripture study, dependence on God, perseverance, cultivating a strong prayer life, engaging in regular Scripture reading, surrounding yourself with fellow believers, and serving others are all vital components of strengthening your faith through life's challenges, leading to a more fulfilling and stress-free life.

Chapter 7: Acquiring the Mind of Christ to Become Biblically Minded

7.1 Understanding the Significance of the Mind of Christ

Acquiring the mind of Christ is essential for Christians seeking to live a biblically minded life. This comprehensive exploration will examine the significance of the mind of Christ and its importance in Christian living, drawing on conservative Christian interpretations.

1. **The Biblical Basis for the Mind of Christ**

The concept of the mind of Christ is derived from various scriptural passages that emphasize the importance of aligning our thoughts, attitudes, and motives with those of Jesus:

a. **Philippians 2:5**: "Let this mind be in you, which was also in Christ Jesus." This verse emphasizes the importance of adopting Christ's mindset of humility and selflessness.

b. **1 Corinthians 2:16**: "For who has known the mind of the Lord, that he may instruct Him? But we have the mind of Christ." This verse highlights the spiritual understanding and wisdom that come from having the mind of Christ.

2. **The Significance of the Mind of Christ**

The mind of Christ holds great significance for Christian living:

a. **Spiritual Maturity**: Acquiring the mind of Christ leads to spiritual maturity, as it enables believers to grow in their understanding of God's will and purpose (Ephesians 4:13-15; Colossians 1:28).

b. **Christ-like Attitude**: Adopting the mind of Christ fosters a Christ-like attitude marked by humility, love, and servanthood (Philippians 2:3-7; John 13:12-17).

c. **Discernment**: Having the mind of Christ equips believers with discernment, enabling them to make wise decisions and choices in accordance with God's Word (Hebrews 5:14; Proverbs 3:5-6).

d. **Biblical Worldview**: Developing the mind of Christ helps believers cultivate a biblical worldview, shaping their thoughts, values, and actions according to Scripture (Romans 12:2; Colossians 3:1-2).

3. Acquiring the Mind of Christ

To acquire the mind of Christ, consider the following biblical principles and practices:

a. **Prayer and Meditation**: Engage in regular prayer and meditation, seeking God's guidance and wisdom (James 1:5; Psalm 119:97-100).

b. **Scripture Study**: Immerse yourself in God's Word, allowing it to transform your thoughts and perspectives (Joshua 1:8; 2 Timothy 3:16-17).

c. **Obedience**: Strive to obey God's commandments and teachings, modeling your life after Jesus (1 John 2:3-6; Luke 9:23).

d. **Fellowship**: Participate in a community of believers, learning from and encouraging one another as you grow in your understanding of Christ's mind (Hebrews 10:24-25; Proverbs 27:17).

Conclusion

Understanding the significance of the mind of Christ is crucial for acquiring a biblically minded life. By embracing the principles of prayer, meditation, Scripture study, obedience, and fellowship, believers can develop the mind of Christ, leading to spiritual maturity, Christ-like attitudes, discernment, and a biblical worldview. Ultimately, having the mind of Christ allows Christians to live in accordance with God's will and purpose, transforming their lives and positively impacting the world around them.

7.2 Delving Deep into God's Word for Transformation

Delving deep into God's Word is essential for believers seeking to acquire the mind of Christ and become biblically minded. This comprehensive exploration will focus on the transformative power of God's Word and its role in shaping the mind of Christ in Christians, drawing on conservative Christian interpretations.

1. The Role of God's Word in Spiritual Transformation

God's Word plays a vital role in spiritual transformation, as it reveals His character, will, and purposes:

a. **Hebrews 4:12**: God's Word is described as living and powerful, capable of discerning the thoughts and intents of the heart. It is an essential tool for spiritual transformation.

b. **2 Timothy 3:16-17**: Scripture is God-breathed and useful for teaching, rebuking, correcting, and training in righteousness, equipping believers for every good work.

c. **Romans 12:2**: The apostle Paul instructs believers not to conform to the pattern of this world but to be transformed by the renewing of their minds through God's Word.

2. Delving Deep into God's Word for Transformation

To delve deep into God's Word for transformation, consider the following biblical principles and practices:

a. **Regular Study**: Engage in regular, systematic study of the Scriptures, seeking to understand and apply God's truth to your life (Psalm 1:1-3; Acts 17:11).

b. **Meditation**: Meditate on God's Word, pondering its meaning and implications for your life (Psalm 119:97-99; Joshua 1:8).

c. **Memorization**: Commit key verses and passages to memory, allowing God's Word to be a constant source of guidance and encouragement (Psalm 119:11; Colossians 3:16).

d. **Application**: Strive to apply God's Word to your daily life, allowing it to shape your thoughts, attitudes, and actions (James 1:22-25; Luke 11:28).

3. The Transformative Power of God's Word

Delving deep into God's Word leads to transformation in various aspects of Christian living:

a. **Renewed Mind**: Studying and meditating on God's Word renews the mind, aligning it with the mind of Christ (Romans 12:2; Ephesians 4:23).

b. **Spiritual Growth**: Immersing oneself in Scripture promotes spiritual growth, equipping believers to discern God's will and mature in their faith (1 Peter 2:2; 2 Peter 3:18).

c. **Discernment**: God's Word provides wisdom and discernment for navigating life's challenges and making God-honoring decisions (Psalm 119:105; Proverbs 2:1-11).

d. **Moral and Ethical Guidance**: Scripture serves as a moral compass, providing guidance for living a life that pleases God (Psalm 119:9-16; 2 Timothy 3:16-17).

Conclusion

Delving deep into God's Word is crucial for acquiring the mind of Christ and becoming biblically minded. Through regular study, meditation, memorization, and application of Scripture, believers can experience the transformative power of God's Word in their lives. This transformation leads to a renewed mind, spiritual growth, discernment, and moral and ethical guidance, enabling Christians to live in accordance with God's will and purpose, reflecting the mind of Christ in their thoughts, attitudes, and actions.

7.3 Cultivating Humility, Love, and Servanthood

Acquiring the mind of Christ involves cultivating humility, love, and servanthood as essential components of biblical living. This comprehensive exploration will draw on conservative Christian interpretations of Scripture to explain how humility, love, and servanthood are interrelated and vital to the development of a Christ-like mindset.

1. **Humility**

Humility is a cornerstone of the Christian life and a fundamental aspect of having the mind of Christ:

a. **Philippians 2:5-8**: The apostle Paul exhorts believers to have the same mindset as Jesus, who humbled Himself, taking on the form of a servant and willingly dying on the cross for our salvation.

b. **Matthew 23:11-12**: Jesus teaches that true greatness is found in humility and service, stating, "The greatest among you will be your servant. Whoever exalts himself will be humbled, and whoever humbles himself will be exalted."

c. **1 Peter 5:5-6**: Believers are encouraged to clothe themselves in humility, submitting to God's mighty hand so that He may exalt them in due time.

2. **Love**

Love is another essential component of the mind of Christ, as it reflects the very nature of God:

a. **1 John 4:7-8**: Believers are called to love one another because love is from God, and God is love.

b. **John 13:34-35**: Jesus commands His disciples to love one another as He has loved them, emphasizing that this love will identify them as His followers.

c. **1 Corinthians 13:1-8**: The apostle Paul highlights the importance of love as the foundation of Christian living, stating that without love, our actions and gifts are meaningless.

3. Servanthood

Servanthood is closely tied to humility and love, reflecting the selflessness and sacrifice of Christ:

a. **Mark 10:42-45**: Jesus teaches that true greatness comes through serving others, exemplifying this principle by pointing to His own life and ministry.

b. **Galatians 5:13-14**: Believers are encouraged to use their freedom in Christ to serve one another in love, fulfilling the law through acts of service.

c. **Ephesians 6:7**: Christians are instructed to serve wholeheartedly, as if serving the Lord, not merely people.

4. Cultivating Humility, Love, and Servanthood

To cultivate humility, love, and servanthood in your life, consider the following practices:

a. **Prayer**: Seek God's help to develop a Christ-like mindset, asking Him to shape your character and heart according to His will (Psalm 139:23-24).

b. **Study and Application**: Study and apply the teachings of Jesus, focusing on His example of humility, love, and servanthood (John 15:9-17; Matthew 20:26-28).

c. **Intentional Acts of Service**: Engage in acts of service for others, both within your faith community and the broader community, as a way of practicing humility and demonstrating love (Galatians 6:10; James 2:14-17).

d. **Fellowship and Accountability**: Cultivate relationships with fellow believers who can encourage and challenge you to grow in humility, love, and servanthood (Hebrews 10:24-25; Proverbs 27:17).

Conclusion

Acquiring the mind of Christ and becoming biblically minded involves cultivating humility, love, and servanthood in our lives. By intentionally pursuing these Christ-like qualities, we align our thoughts, attitudes, and actions with those of Jesus. This transformative process enables us to more fully experience and embody God's kingdom here on earth, impacting not only our own lives but also the lives of those around us.

As we immerse ourselves in God's Word, seek His guidance through prayer, serve others in love, and engage in meaningful fellowship with fellow believers, we can develop the mind of Christ and become more biblically minded. In doing so, we will grow in spiritual maturity and become more effective witnesses of God's love, grace, and truth in a world that desperately needs the hope and healing found in Jesus Christ.

7.4 Embracing a Prayerful and Spirit-Led Life

Embracing a prayerful and Spirit-led life is crucial for acquiring the mind of Christ and becoming biblically minded. Through prayer and the guidance of the Holy Spirit, we can develop an intimate relationship with God, align our will with His, and experience transformation in our thoughts, attitudes, and actions. This comprehensive exploration will draw on conservative Christian interpretations of Scripture to explain the importance of a prayerful and Spirit-led life in cultivating the mind of Christ.

1. **Prayer**

Prayer plays a vital role in connecting with God and acquiring the mind of Christ:

a. **Philippians 4:6-7**: Believers are encouraged to present their requests to God through prayer, which leads to God's peace guarding their hearts and minds in Christ Jesus.

b. **Colossians 4:2**: Christians are instructed to devote themselves to prayer, being watchful and thankful.

c. **Matthew 6:9-13**: Jesus teaches His disciples to pray, providing a model that emphasizes the centrality of God's will, the provision of daily needs, and forgiveness.

2. The Holy Spirit

The Holy Spirit is essential in guiding believers towards a biblically minded life:

a. **John 14:26**: Jesus promises the Holy Spirit as the Counselor, who will teach believers all things and remind them of His teachings.

b. **Romans 8:26-27**: The Holy Spirit helps believers in their weakness, interceding on their behalf according to God's will.

c. **Galatians 5:16-25**: Believers are instructed to live by the Spirit, allowing the Spirit to guide their lives and produce the fruit of the Spirit, which includes love, joy, peace, patience, kindness, goodness, faithfulness, gentleness, and self-control.

3. Embracing a Prayerful and Spirit-Led Life

To embrace a prayerful and Spirit-led life, consider the following practices:

a. **Consistent Prayer**: Develop a habit of regular prayer, setting aside dedicated time for conversation with God (1 Thessalonians 5:17).

b. **Listening**: Be still and listen for the Holy Spirit's guidance during prayer and throughout your day (Psalm 46:10).

c. **Scripture Meditation**: Meditate on God's Word, allowing the Holy Spirit to reveal its meaning and application in your life (Joshua 1:8; Psalm 1:2).

d. **Surrender**: Submit your will to God, asking the Holy Spirit to lead you in all aspects of your life (Proverbs 3:5-6).

e. **Fellowship**: Engage with fellow believers, sharing your prayer requests and experiences of the Holy Spirit's guidance (James 5:16; Hebrews 10:24-25).

Conclusion

Acquiring the mind of Christ and becoming biblically minded requires embracing a prayerful and Spirit-led life. Through consistent prayer and reliance on the Holy Spirit's guidance, we can deepen our relationship with God, align our will with His, and experience transformation in our thoughts, attitudes, and actions. By actively pursuing a prayerful and Spirit-led life, we can cultivate the mind of Christ and become more effective witnesses of God's love, grace, and truth in the world.

7.5 Practicing Discernment and Applying Biblical Wisdom

Practicing discernment and applying biblical wisdom are essential components of acquiring the mind of Christ and becoming biblically minded. Discernment enables believers to differentiate between God's truth and worldly influences, while biblical wisdom provides guidance for living a life that honors God. This comprehensive exploration will draw on conservative Christian interpretations of Scripture to explain the importance of discernment and the application of biblical wisdom in cultivating the mind of Christ.

1. **Discernment**

Discernment is a critical skill for believers seeking to acquire the mind of Christ:

a. **Hebrews 5:14**: Mature believers should have trained themselves to distinguish good from evil through constant practice.

b. **1 John 4:1**: Christians are instructed to test the spirits to see if they are from God, as many false prophets have gone into the world.

c. **Proverbs 2:2-5**: Believers are encouraged to seek wisdom, understanding, and discernment by attentively listening to God's words and applying their hearts to understanding.

2. **Biblical Wisdom**

Biblical wisdom provides guidance for living a Christ-centered life:

a. **Proverbs 1:7**: The fear of the Lord is the beginning of knowledge, and wisdom starts with a proper reverence for God.

b. **James 1:5**: Believers who lack wisdom should ask God, who gives generously to all without reproach, and it will be given to them.

c. **Colossians 3:16**: Christians are instructed to let the word of Christ dwell in them richly, teaching and admonishing one another in all wisdom.

3. Practicing Discernment and Applying Biblical Wisdom

To practice discernment and apply biblical wisdom, consider the following steps:

a. **Study Scripture**: Immerse yourself in God's Word, gaining a thorough understanding of its teachings to help you discern truth from falsehood (2 Timothy 2:15).

b. **Pray for Wisdom**: Ask God for wisdom and discernment in your daily life, trusting that He will provide the insight you need (James 1:5).

c. **Seek Godly Counsel**: Consult with trusted fellow believers who can offer biblical advice and guidance in various situations (Proverbs 15:22).

d. **Examine Your Motivations**: Regularly evaluate your intentions and motives to ensure they align with God's will and the teachings of Scripture (2 Corinthians 13:5).

e. **Be Watchful**: Stay alert to potential deception, false teachings, or worldly influences that could distract you from God's truth (1 Peter 5:8).

Conclusion

Acquiring the mind of Christ and becoming biblically minded requires practicing discernment and applying biblical wisdom. By studying Scripture, praying for wisdom, seeking godly counsel, examining our motivations, and being watchful, we can develop the discernment and wisdom needed to live a Christ-centered life. As we grow in discernment and wisdom, we cultivate the mind of Christ and become more effective witnesses of God's love, grace, and truth in the world.

7.6 Fostering Christlike Character and Virtues

Fostering Christlike character and virtues is an essential part of acquiring the mind of Christ and becoming biblically minded. By cultivating virtues such as love, humility, patience, and self-control, believers can emulate Jesus' character and live in accordance with God's will. This comprehensive exploration will draw on conservative Christian interpretations of Scripture to explain the importance of nurturing Christlike character and virtues in the pursuit of acquiring the mind of Christ.

1. **Love**

Love is the most significant virtue and the foundation of all other Christlike characteristics:

a. **Matthew 22:37-40**: Jesus emphasizes the importance of love by stating that the two greatest commandments are to love God and love others.

b. **1 Corinthians 13:4-7**: The Apostle Paul describes the characteristics of love, emphasizing its centrality in a believer's life.

c. John 13:34-35: Jesus instructs His followers to love one another as He has loved them, stating that this love will demonstrate to the world that they are His disciples.

2. **Humility**

Humility is a core virtue in emulating Christ's character:

a. **Philippians 2:5-8**: Paul encourages believers to adopt the attitude of Christ, who humbled Himself and became obedient to death on the cross.

b. **1 Peter 5:5-6**: Believers are instructed to clothe themselves with humility, submitting to one another and humbling themselves before God.

c. **Proverbs 22:4**: Humility is connected to the fear of the Lord and leads to riches, honor, and life.

3. **Patience and Self-Control**

Patience and self-control are essential virtues in cultivating Christlike character:

a. **Galatians 5:22-23**: Patience and self-control are listed among the fruits of the Spirit, which are produced in believers' lives as they walk in the Spirit.

b. **James 1:2-4**: James encourages believers to view trials as opportunities to develop perseverance and mature character.

c. **Proverbs 25:28**: A person without self-control is compared to a city with broken walls, indicating the importance of maintaining self-control for a believer.

4. **Fostering Christlike Character and Virtues**

To foster Christlike character and virtues, consider the following steps:

a. **Study Scripture**: Immerse yourself in God's Word, learning about the character and virtues of Christ and how they can be reflected in your life (Romans 12:2).

b. **Pray for Transformation**: Ask God to help you develop Christlike virtues and to transform your heart and mind (Philippians 4:6-7).

c. **Practice Spiritual Disciplines**: Engage in practices such as prayer, meditation, fasting, and worship to cultivate your relationship with God and grow in Christlike character (1 Timothy 4:7-8).

d. **Be Accountable**: Seek accountability from fellow believers, who can encourage you and help you stay on track in your pursuit of Christlikeness (Hebrews 10:24-25).

e. **Persevere**: Continue striving to grow in Christlike character, trusting that God is at work in you to complete His good work (Philippians 1:6).

Conclusion

Acquiring the mind of Christ and becoming biblically minded involves fostering Christlike character and virtues such as love, humility, patience, and self-control. By studying Scripture, praying for transformation, practicing spiritual disciplines, seeking accountability, and persevering, believers can cultivate Christlike character and virtues, allowing them to make decisions that have a greater opportunity of success.

Chapter 8: Do Not Allow Your Circumstances to Control Your Life

8.1 Embracing God's Sovereignty Over Circumstances

As believers, it is essential to embrace God's sovereignty over circumstances and not allow them to control our lives. Trusting in God's sovereignty enables us to experience peace, hope, and joy, even in the most challenging situations. This comprehensive exploration will draw on conservative Christian interpretations of Scripture to explain the importance of embracing God's sovereignty over circumstances.

1. **God's Sovereignty**

God's sovereignty means that He is in complete control of all aspects of creation, including our lives and circumstances:

a. **Psalm 103:19**: The Lord's throne is in heaven, and He exercises sovereignty over all.

b. **Proverbs 16:33**: Even seemingly random events are under God's control.

c. **Romans 8:28**: God works all things together for the good of those who love Him and are called according to His purpose.

2. **Trusting in God's Sovereignty**

Trusting in God's sovereignty over circumstances involves acknowledging His control and submitting to His will:

a. **Proverbs 3:5-6**: Believers are instructed to trust in the Lord with all their hearts, acknowledging Him in all their ways, and He will direct their paths.

b. **Isaiah 26:3-4**: God promises to keep in perfect peace those whose minds are steadfast because they trust in Him.

c. **Matthew 6:25-34**: Jesus teaches His followers not to worry about their lives or material needs but to seek first God's kingdom and righteousness, trusting that He will provide for them.

3. Responding to Circumstances with Faith and Obedience

Embracing God's sovereignty over circumstances involves responding with faith and obedience:

a. **James 1:2-4**: Believers are encouraged to consider trials as opportunities for joy, knowing that testing produces perseverance and mature character.

b. **Philippians 4:6-7**: In every situation, believers should present their requests to God through prayer and thanksgiving, and God's peace will guard their hearts and minds in Christ Jesus.

c. **Romans 12:1-2**: Believers are called to offer their lives as living sacrifices to God, allowing their minds to be transformed and discerning God's will in their circumstances.

4. Maintaining a God-Centered Perspective

To embrace God's sovereignty over circumstances, cultivate a God-centered perspective:

a. **Colossians 3:1-4**: Believers should set their hearts and minds on things above, where Christ is seated at the right hand of God, rather than on earthly concerns.

b. **2 Corinthians 4:16-18**: Though believers may face hardships, they should focus on the eternal glory that outweighs their temporary afflictions.

c. **Hebrews 12:1-2**: Believers should fix their eyes on Jesus, the author and perfecter of their faith, who endured the cross for the joy set before Him.

Conclusion

Embracing God's sovereignty over circumstances is essential for believers to maintain peace, hope, and joy in their lives. By trusting in God's control, submitting to His will, responding to circumstances with faith and obedience, and maintaining a God-centered perspective, believers can prevent their circumstances from controlling their lives and experience the fullness of God's love and provision.

8.2 Practicing Mindfulness and Acceptance

Although mindfulness and acceptance are concepts often associated with Eastern practices, there are biblical principles that can help believers practice mindfulness and acceptance in a conservative Christian context. By focusing on the present moment and accepting reality, believers can find peace and trust in God's plan for their lives, regardless of their circumstances.

1. **Be Present in the Moment**

The Bible emphasizes the importance of living in the present and not being consumed by worries about the future:

a. **Matthew 6:34**: Jesus instructs His followers not to worry about tomorrow, as each day has enough trouble of its own.

b. **Psalm 118:24**: The psalmist declares that this is the day the Lord has made and encourages rejoicing and gladness.

c. **Philippians 4:8**: Believers are instructed to think about whatever is true, noble, right, pure, lovely, and admirable, promoting a focus on the present moment.

2. **Acceptance of Reality**

Accepting reality means acknowledging and embracing the circumstances God has allowed in our lives:

a. **Romans 8:28**: God works all things together for the good of those who love Him and are called according to His purpose.

b. **Proverbs 3:5-6**: Trusting in God's sovereignty involves accepting the reality He allows and submitting to His will.

c. **2 Corinthians 12:9-10**: Paul accepts his "thorn in the flesh," finding strength in his weakness as Christ's power is made perfect.

3. Cultivating a Heart of Contentment

Learning to be content in every situation can help believers find peace and acceptance:

a. **Philippians 4:11-13**: Paul writes that he has learned to be content in any circumstance, relying on Christ who strengthens him.

b. **1 Timothy 6:6-8**: Contentment with godliness is considered great gain, and believers are encouraged to be satisfied with basic necessities.

c. **Hebrews 13:5**: Believers are reminded to be content with what they have, as God has promised never to leave nor forsake them.

4. Practicing Gratitude

Gratitude can be a helpful practice in developing mindfulness and acceptance:

a. **1 Thessalonians 5:16-18**: Believers are encouraged to give thanks in all circumstances, as this is God's will for them in Christ Jesus.

b. **Ephesians 5:20**: Believers should give thanks to God the Father for everything in the name of Jesus Christ.

c. **Colossians 3:17**: In word and deed, believers should give thanks to God through Jesus Christ.

Conclusion

Practicing mindfulness and acceptance in a biblically-based and conservative Christian context involves being present in the moment, accepting reality, cultivating contentment, and expressing gratitude. By focusing on these principles, believers can prevent their circumstances from controlling their lives and experience the peace and joy that come from trusting in God's plan.

8.3 Building Resilience Through Spiritual Growth

Building resilience through spiritual growth enables believers to navigate life's challenges without allowing circumstances to control them. By developing a deep relationship with God, embracing His Word, and relying on the Holy Spirit, believers can cultivate a strong foundation that withstands life's trials.

1. **Developing a Deep Relationship with God**

A deep relationship with God is the cornerstone of spiritual growth and resilience:

a. **Psalm 46:1-3**: God is our refuge and strength, an ever-present help in times of trouble.

b. **Proverbs 18:10**: The name of the Lord is a strong tower; the righteous run to it and are safe.

c. **James 4:8**: When believers draw near to God, He draws near to them, providing strength and refuge in times of need.

2. **Embracing God's Word**

Meditating on and internalizing God's Word is essential for spiritual growth and resilience:

a. **Psalm 119:105**: God's Word is a lamp to our feet and a light to our path, guiding us through life's challenges.

b. **2 Timothy 3:16-17**: Scripture is useful for teaching, rebuking, correcting, and training in righteousness, equipping believers for every good work.

c. **Romans 15:4**: The Scriptures provide encouragement and hope, strengthening believers in difficult times.

3. **Relying on the Holy Spirit**

The Holy Spirit plays a crucial role in spiritual growth and resilience:

a. **John 14:26**: The Holy Spirit teaches and reminds believers of all that Jesus has said, providing guidance and wisdom.

b. **Romans 8:26-27**: The Holy Spirit intercedes for believers in their weakness, aligning their prayers with God's will.

c. **Galatians 5:22-23**: The Holy Spirit produces spiritual fruit in believers, including love, joy, peace, patience, kindness, goodness, faithfulness, gentleness, and self-control.

4. Building a Supportive Faith Community

A supportive faith community is essential for spiritual growth and resilience:

a. **Hebrews 10:24-25**: Believers are encouraged to meet together regularly to spur one another on to love and good deeds.

b. **Ecclesiastes 4:9-12**: A strong support system provides encouragement, strength, and protection during times of difficulty.

c. **Galatians 6:2**: Believers are called to bear one another's burdens, fulfilling the law of Christ.

Conclusion

Building resilience through spiritual growth involves developing a deep relationship with God, embracing His Word, relying on the Holy Spirit, and fostering a supportive faith community. By nurturing these aspects of their spiritual lives, believers can prevent circumstances from controlling their lives and experience the peace, strength, and hope that come from a strong foundation in Christ.

8.4 Cultivating a Positive and God-Centered Mindset

Cultivating a positive and God-centered mindset is essential for believers who want to prevent their circumstances from controlling their lives. By focusing on God's truth, trusting in His promises, and practicing gratitude, believers can maintain a hopeful and optimistic perspective, regardless of their circumstances.

1. **Focusing on God's Truth**

Grounding oneself in God's truth is crucial for developing a positive and God-centered mindset:

a. **Philippians 4:8**: Believers are encouraged to think about whatever is true, noble, right, pure, lovely, admirable, excellent, and praiseworthy.

b. **Isaiah 26:3**: God promises to keep those whose minds are steadfast on Him in perfect peace.

c. **John 8:32**: Jesus said that knowing the truth would set believers free, allowing them to rise above their circumstances.

2. **Trusting in God's Promises**

Believers can maintain a positive and God-centered mindset by trusting in God's promises:

a. **Romans 8:28**: God works all things together for the good of those who love Him and are called according to His purpose.

b. **Matthew 6:33**: Jesus encourages believers to seek first God's kingdom and His righteousness, with the assurance that their needs will be provided for.

c. **Isaiah 41:10**: God promises to strengthen, help, and uphold believers with His righteous right hand.

3. **Practicing Gratitude**

Gratitude is essential for cultivating a positive and God-centered mindset:

a. **1 Thessalonians 5:16-18**: Believers are instructed to rejoice always, pray continually, and give thanks in all circumstances, for this is God's will for them in Christ Jesus.

b. **Psalm 136:1-3**: Offering thanks to God for His steadfast love and faithfulness can shift one's focus from their circumstances to God's goodness.

c. **Colossians 3:15-17**: Believers are encouraged to let the peace of Christ rule in their hearts and express gratitude to God in word and deed.

4. Relying on the Holy Spirit

The Holy Spirit plays a vital role in cultivating a positive and God-centered mindset:

a. **Romans 12:2**: Believers are called to be transformed by the renewing of their minds, which is accomplished through the Holy Spirit's work.

b. **Galatians 5:22-23**: The Holy Spirit produces spiritual fruit in believers, including love, joy, and peace, which contribute to a positive mindset.

c. **John 16:13**: The Holy Spirit guides believers into all truth, helping them maintain a God-centered perspective.

Conclusion

Cultivating a positive and God-centered mindset involves focusing on God's truth, trusting in His promises, practicing gratitude, and relying on the Holy Spirit. By adopting these practices, believers can prevent their circumstances from controlling their lives and experience the joy, peace, and hope that come from a close relationship with God.

8.5 Setting Healthy Boundaries and Priorities

Setting healthy boundaries and priorities is crucial for believers who want to prevent their circumstances from controlling their lives. By learning to say 'no' when necessary, focusing on God-given priorities, and making time for rest and spiritual growth, believers can maintain a balanced life that honors God.

1. Learning to Say 'No'

Scripture encourages believers to establish boundaries and be discerning in their commitments:

a. **Matthew 5:37**: Jesus teaches that one's 'yes' should mean 'yes' and 'no' should mean 'no,' emphasizing the importance of clear communication and decision-making.

b. **Proverbs 4:23**: Believers are instructed to guard their hearts diligently, as it affects all aspects of life.

c. **Galatians 6:5**: Each person should carry their own load, recognizing that it is essential to set boundaries to avoid being overburdened.

2. **Focusing on God-Given Priorities**

Aligning one's priorities with God's will is essential for maintaining balance and preventing circumstances from controlling one's life:

a. **Matthew 6:33**: Jesus instructs believers to seek first the kingdom of God and His righteousness, indicating the importance of prioritizing God's will.

b. **Colossians 3:23-24**: Believers are called to work heartily in whatever they do, as unto the Lord, recognizing that their ultimate priority is to please Him.

c. **Ephesians 5:15-17**: Believers should be wise, making the most of their time, and discerning God's will in their lives.

3. **Making Time for Rest and Spiritual Growth**

Ensuring adequate rest and spiritual growth is essential for maintaining a healthy, God-centered life:

a. **Mark 6:31**: Jesus invited His disciples to come away and rest after a period of ministry, emphasizing the importance of balance and self-care.

b. **Psalm 23:2-3**: God leads His people beside still waters and restores their souls, indicating the necessity of rest and spiritual renewal.

c. **Hebrews 4:9-11**: Believers are encouraged to enter into God's rest, which represents the spiritual rest that comes from trusting in Christ's finished work.

4. Cultivating Godly Relationships

Believers should prioritize relationships that promote spiritual growth and accountability:

a. **Proverbs 27:17**: As iron sharpens iron, so one person sharpens another, illustrating the importance of godly friendships.

b. **Ecclesiastes 4:9-12**: Scripture highlights the benefits of companionship, support, and accountability in relationships.

c. **Hebrews 10:24-25**: Believers are encouraged to gather together for mutual encouragement and to spur one another toward love and good deeds.

Conclusion

Setting healthy boundaries and priorities helps believers prevent their circumstances from controlling their lives. By learning to say 'no,' focusing on God-given priorities, making time for rest and spiritual growth, and cultivating godly relationships, believers can live a balanced life that honors God and promotes spiritual well-being.

8.6 Turning Challenges into Opportunities for Growth

Facing challenges is an inevitable part of life, and believers can turn these challenges into opportunities for growth by embracing God's sovereignty, learning from trials, relying on God's strength, and encouraging others through their experiences.

1. Embracing God's Sovereignty

Recognizing that God is in control of every situation can help believers transform challenges into opportunities for growth:

    a. **Romans 8:28**: God works all things together for good for those who love Him and are called according to His purpose, affirming His sovereignty in all circumstances.

    b. **Isaiah 55:8-9**: God's thoughts and ways are higher than ours, indicating that He has a greater perspective and plan in the midst of challenges.

    c. **Job 42:2**: Job acknowledged God's sovereignty and power after facing numerous trials, demonstrating the importance of trusting in God's control.

    2. **Learning from Trials**

Challenges can teach believers valuable lessons and refine their character:

    a. **James 1:2-4**: Believers are encouraged to consider it pure joy when they face trials, as the testing of their faith produces perseverance and spiritual maturity.

    b. **Romans 5:3-5**: Suffering produces perseverance, character, and hope, revealing that challenges can lead to growth.

    c. **1 Peter 1:6-7**: Trials test the genuineness of one's faith, refining it like gold in a fire, highlighting the value of learning from challenges.

    3. **Relying on God's Strength**

Believers can turn challenges into opportunities for growth by depending on God's strength and grace:

    a. **2 Corinthians 12:9-10**: God's grace is sufficient for believers, and His power is made perfect in weakness, reminding us to rely on His strength in difficult times.

    b. **Philippians 4:13**: Paul declared that he could do all things through Christ who strengthens him, emphasizing the importance of depending on God during challenges.

    c. **Isaiah 40:31**: Those who wait upon the Lord will renew their strength and soar on wings like eagles, illustrating the benefits of relying on God's power.

4. Encouraging Others through Experiences

Sharing personal experiences and supporting others in their challenges can lead to growth and spiritual development:

a. **2 Corinthians 1:3-4**: God comforts believers in their afflictions so that they may comfort others who are experiencing similar difficulties, highlighting the value of sharing experiences.

b. **Galatians 6:2**: Believers are called to bear one another's burdens, fulfilling the law of Christ, and demonstrating the importance of supporting others during challenges.

c. **1 Thessalonians 5:11**: Believers are encouraged to build one another up, emphasizing the role of encouragement in spiritual growth.

Conclusion

Believers can turn challenges into opportunities for growth by embracing God's sovereignty, learning from trials, relying on His strength, and encouraging others through their experiences. By adopting this mindset, Christians can prevent their circumstances from controlling their lives and instead leverage them for spiritual growth and development.

Chapter 9: Cling to Your Faith Regardless of the Trial You Face

9.1 Strengthening Your Trust in God's Plan

Maintaining faith during trials is crucial for believers, as it allows them to grow spiritually, experience God's presence, and witness His transformative power. By strengthening their trust in God's plan, believers can persevere through challenges with unwavering faith and hope.

1. **Recognizing God's Sovereignty**

Understanding that God is in control and has a purpose for every situation can help believers maintain faith during trials:

a. **Proverbs 3:5-6**: Trusting in the Lord with all our heart and acknowledging Him in all our ways enables Him to direct our paths, confirming His sovereignty over our lives.

b. **Isaiah 41:10**: God encourages believers not to fear or be dismayed, as He will strengthen and uphold them, highlighting His control in every circumstance.

c. **Jeremiah 29:11**: God has plans to prosper and not to harm His people, providing hope and a future, assuring believers of His intentions.

2. **Learning from Scripture**

Scripture offers numerous examples of faith and trust in God's plan, providing guidance and inspiration for believers during trials:

a. **Hebrews 11**: The "Hall of Faith" chapter highlights examples of individuals who trusted in God's plan despite various challenges, demonstrating the importance of maintaining faith during trials.

b. **Job**: Despite immense suffering, Job clung to his faith in God, ultimately experiencing restoration and blessing as a result of his unwavering trust in God's plan.

c. **Paul**: The Apostle Paul faced numerous hardships but remained faithful and committed to God's purpose for his life, providing a powerful example of perseverance.

3. **Engaging in Prayer and Worship**

Prayer and worship can strengthen a believer's trust in God's plan during trials:

a. **Philippians 4:6-7**: Praying with thanksgiving in all circumstances brings peace that surpasses understanding, enabling believers to trust in God's plan.

b. **Psalm 34:1-3**: Worshiping and praising God during trials can help shift focus from the situation to God's goodness and faithfulness, fostering trust in His plan.

c. **1 Peter 5:7**: Casting all anxieties on God because He cares for us highlights the importance of relying on Him during trials and trusting in His plan.

4. **Cultivating a Supportive Faith Community**

A strong faith community can help believers cling to their faith during trials:

a. **Ecclesiastes 4:9-12**: A supportive community can provide encouragement, strength, and accountability during challenging times, enabling believers to maintain their faith.

b. **Hebrews 10:24-25**: Believers are encouraged to meet together for mutual encouragement, reinforcing the importance of a supportive faith community.

c. **Galatians 6:2**: Bearing one another's burdens helps believers persevere through trials, fostering spiritual growth and strengthening faith.

Conclusion

Clinging to faith regardless of the trial requires recognizing God's sovereignty, learning from Scripture, engaging in prayer and worship, and cultivating a supportive faith community. By strengthening their trust in God's plan, believers can face challenges with unwavering faith and confidence, experiencing God's transformative power and presence in their lives.

9.2 Harnessing the Power of Prayer During Trials

During trials, prayer is an essential aspect of maintaining faith and drawing closer to God. Through prayer, believers can find comfort, strength, and guidance from the Lord, enabling them to persevere and ultimately experience His transformative power in their lives.

1. **Seeking Comfort and Peace in Prayer**

Prayer can provide believers with a sense of comfort and peace during trials:

a. **Philippians 4:6-7**: Believers are encouraged to bring their concerns to God in prayer, allowing His peace to guard their hearts and minds.

b. **Psalm 62:8**: Pouring out our hearts to God in prayer can provide relief and solace during difficult times, as He is a refuge for the soul.

c. **Matthew 11:28-30**: Jesus invites the weary and burdened to come to Him, promising rest and peace through prayer and communion with Him.

2. **Receiving Strength and Courage Through Prayer**

Prayer can empower believers with the strength and courage needed to face trials:

a. **Isaiah 40:29-31**: God promises to renew the strength of those who hope in Him, allowing them to rise above their trials.

b. **Ephesians 6:18**: Persistent and continuous prayer empowers believers to stand firm against spiritual attacks during trials.

c. **2 Corinthians 12:9-10**: Paul acknowledges that God's power is made perfect in weakness, and by relying on God through prayer, believers can find strength in times of trial.

3. Seeking God's Guidance and Wisdom

Prayer allows believers to seek God's guidance and wisdom during trials:

a. **James 1:5**: God generously provides wisdom to those who ask in faith, enabling believers to navigate trials with divine understanding.

b. **Proverbs 3:5-6**: Trusting in the Lord and acknowledging Him in all our ways ensures that He will direct our paths, even during challenging times.

c. **John 16:13**: The Holy Spirit, our helper and guide, can lead believers in truth and provide guidance during trials.

4. Intercessory Prayer and Support

Believers can harness the power of prayer by interceding for one another during trials:

a. **Colossians 1:9-12**: Paul's intercessory prayers for the Colossian church demonstrate the importance of praying for spiritual growth, understanding, and strength for fellow believers during trials.

b. **Galatians 6:2**: Bearing one another's burdens through prayer is an essential aspect of Christian fellowship and support.

c. **1 Timothy 2:1-2**: Believers are encouraged to pray for others, including those in authority, as an expression of love and concern during trials.

Conclusion

Clinging to faith during trials involves harnessing the power of prayer to seek comfort, peace, strength, courage, guidance, and wisdom from God. Additionally, intercessory prayer and support from fellow believers can provide encouragement and hope. Through prayer, believers can experience God's presence, love, and transformative power, enabling them to persevere through trials and grow in their faith.

9.3 Learning from Biblical Examples of Perseverance

Throughout the Bible, various individuals exemplify perseverance through trials and tribulations. These examples can inspire and encourage believers to maintain their faith during difficult times. By studying these biblical characters, believers can learn valuable lessons about trusting God, seeking His guidance, and relying on His strength.

1. **Esther: Courage and Trust in God's Sovereignty**

The story of Esther showcases her courage and trust in God's sovereignty as she risked her life to save her people from destruction:

a. **Esther 4:14-16**: Despite the risks, Esther chose to approach the king on behalf of her people, trusting in God's plan and relying on His guidance.

b. Esther's courage and faith in God's sovereignty provide a powerful example of perseverance during trials, demonstrating the importance of trusting in God's plan and purpose.

2. **Daniel**: Unwavering Faith and Commitment to God

Daniel's unwavering faith and commitment to God in the face of adversity demonstrate the importance of perseverance during trials:

a. **Daniel 6:10-23**: Despite knowing the consequences, Daniel continued to pray to God and was thrown into the lions' den. God protected and delivered him, showcasing His faithfulness to those who remain committed to Him.

b. Daniel's story illustrates the importance of remaining steadfast in faith, even when faced with persecution or opposition.

3. **Hannah**: Perseverance in Prayer and Trust in God's Timing

Hannah's perseverance in prayer and trust in God's timing highlight the importance of patience and faith during trials:

a. **1 Samuel 1:9-20**: Despite years of barrenness and heartache, Hannah continued to pray earnestly for a child. In time, God answered her prayer, blessing her with a son, Samuel.

b. Hannah's story teaches believers to persevere in prayer, trusting in God's timing and faithfulness to fulfill His promises.

4. **Joseph**: Maintaining Integrity and Trusting God's Plan

Joseph's life demonstrates the importance of maintaining integrity and trusting God's plan, even during the most challenging circumstances:

a. **Genesis 37, 39-45**: Joseph faced betrayal, false accusations, and imprisonment, yet he continued to trust in God and maintain his integrity. Ultimately, God used these trials to elevate Joseph to a position of authority, allowing him to save his family during a famine.

b. Joseph's story underscores the importance of trusting in God's plan, even when circumstances seem bleak or unjust.

5. **Job**: Faithfulness and Perseverance Amidst Suffering

Job's faithfulness and perseverance amidst immense suffering provide a powerful example of maintaining faith during trials:

a. **Job 1-2, 42**: Despite losing his wealth, family, and health, Job remained faithful to God. In the end, God restored Job's fortunes and blessed him with even greater prosperity.

b. Job's story teaches believers the importance of remaining faithful to God, even during intense suffering and loss, as God is ultimately in control and can bring restoration and blessing.

Conclusion

By examining the lives of Esther, Daniel, Hannah, Joseph, and Job, believers can learn valuable lessons about perseverance during trials. These biblical examples demonstrate the importance of trusting in God's sovereignty, maintaining faith and commitment, praying persistently, upholding integrity, and remaining faithful during suffering. By applying these principles, believers can find strength and encouragement to cling to their faith, regardless of the trials they face.

9.4 Nurturing Hope and Encouragement Through God's Word

God's Word is a powerful source of hope and encouragement for believers facing trials and difficulties. By studying and meditating on the Scriptures, Christians can find strength, comfort, and guidance to persevere in their faith, regardless of the challenges they encounter.

1. **God's Promises Provide Hope**

The Bible is filled with God's promises that offer hope and encouragement during difficult times:

a. **Hebrews 13:5**: God promises to never leave or forsake His people, providing assurance of His constant presence and support.

b. **Romans 8:28**: The promise that God works all things for the good of those who love Him and are called according to His purpose provides hope that He can use even the most challenging circumstances for our benefit.

2. **God's Word Offers Comfort and Encouragement**

Scripture is a source of comfort and encouragement for believers facing trials:

a. **Psalm 23**: The Lord is portrayed as a shepherd who cares for His sheep, providing comfort, guidance, and protection.

b. **Isaiah 40:31**: Those who hope in the Lord are promised renewed strength, enabling them to persevere through difficulties.

3. **The Bible Equips Believers for Spiritual Growth**

God's Word provides guidance and instruction for spiritual growth during trials:

a. **James 1:2-4**: Trials are seen as opportunities for growth, developing perseverance and maturity in believers.

b. **2 Corinthians 4:16-18**: Believers are encouraged to focus on eternal, spiritual realities rather than temporary, earthly circumstances.

4. Scripture Encourages Believers to Trust God

The Bible encourages believers to trust God during trials and difficulties:

a. **Proverbs 3:5-6**: Trusting in the Lord and acknowledging Him in all our ways promises guidance and direction.

b. **Matthew 6:25-34**: Jesus teaches His followers not to worry about their lives, but to trust in God's provision and care.

5. God's Word Provides Examples of Faith and Perseverance

Scripture is filled with examples of faith and perseverance, inspiring believers to cling to their faith during trials:

a. **Hebrews 11**: Hebrews 11 is a chapter in the New Testament book of Hebrews that is commonly known as the "Faith Chapter" or the "Hall of Faith." It is a collection of stories of men and women who demonstrated great faith in God and His promises, even in the face of adversity and uncertainty. The chapter begins by defining faith as the assurance of things hoped for, the conviction of things not seen. It then goes on to list several examples of faith from the Old Testament, starting with Abel, the son of Adam and Eve, and ending with the prophet Samuel. Each example illustrates a different aspect of faith, from Abel's sacrifice, which demonstrated his faith in God's forgiveness, to Rahab's hospitality to the Israelite spies, which showed her faith in their God. The chapter also emphasizes the importance of faith in pleasing God, stating that "without faith, it is impossible to please him" (Hebrews 11:6).

b. **2 Corinthians 11:23-29**: The Apostle Paul shares his own experiences of trials and hardships, offering encouragement to believers facing difficulties.

Conclusion

The Bible is a powerful source of hope, encouragement, and guidance for believers facing trials and difficulties. By turning to God's Word, Christians can find strength, comfort, and direction to persevere in their faith, regardless of the challenges they face. Through God's promises, examples of faith and perseverance, and the teachings of Jesus, believers can nurture hope and encouragement, clinging to their faith in the midst of trials.

9.5 Embracing the Role of Community and Support

The Bible emphasizes the importance of community and support in the life of a believer, particularly during times of trial and adversity. By engaging with fellow believers and leaning on one another for encouragement, strength, and guidance, Christians can find the support they need to persevere in their faith through life's challenges.

1. **The Importance of Fellowship and Community**

The New Testament highlights the importance of fellowship and community in the early church:

a. **Acts 2:42-47**: The early believers devoted themselves to the apostles' teaching, fellowship, breaking of bread, and prayer. They supported one another and shared their possessions to meet the needs of the community.

b. **Hebrews 10:24-25**: Believers are encouraged to meet together regularly to encourage one another and build each other up in the faith.

2. **The Role of Encouragement and Support**

The Bible stresses the importance of encouragement and support within the Christian community:

a. **1 Thessalonians 5:11**: Believers are instructed to encourage and build each other up, providing support during times of trial.

b. **Galatians 6:2**: Christians are called to "bear one another's burdens," offering help and support to those who are struggling.

3. The Power of Prayer and Intercession

Prayer is a vital aspect of community support during times of trial:

a. **James 5:16**: Believers are instructed to pray for one another, recognizing the power of prayer to bring healing and restoration.

b. **Colossians 4:2-4**: The Apostle Paul asks for prayer from fellow believers as he faces trials and difficulties in his ministry.

4. Spiritual Growth Through Mutual Edification

Believers can experience spiritual growth and encouragement through mutual edification within the community:

a. **Ephesians 4:15-16**: As each member of the body of Christ supports and encourages one another, the entire community grows stronger in faith and unity.

b. **Proverbs 27:17**: "As iron sharpens iron, so one person sharpens another" illustrates the importance of mutual support and encouragement for spiritual growth.

5. The Ministry of Comfort and Support

The Bible highlights the importance of offering comfort and support to others who are facing trials:

a. **2 Corinthians 1:3-4**: God is described as the "Father of compassion" and the "God of all comfort," who comforts us in our troubles so that we may comfort others with the same comfort we have received.

b. **Romans 12:15**: Believers are instructed to "rejoice with those who rejoice, and weep with those who weep," demonstrating empathy and support for one another.

Conclusion

In times of trial and adversity, it is crucial for Christians to embrace the role of community and support. By engaging in fellowship, offering encouragement and prayer, and seeking spiritual growth through mutual edification, believers can find the strength and resilience needed to cling to their faith, regardless of the challenges they face. As the body of Christ, we are called to support and uplift one another, providing comfort and care in the midst of life's difficulties.

9.6 Growing in Faith Through Every Season of Life

Life is full of different seasons, each presenting unique challenges and opportunities for growth. As Christians, our faith should not be static, but rather, should continually grow and mature as we navigate the various stages of life. The Bible provides guidance on how to cling to your faith regardless of the trial you face and grow in faith through every season of life.

1. Trusting God in All Circumstances

In every season, we must learn to trust God and rely on His promises:

a. **Proverbs 3:5-6**: This passage is a call to trust in God completely and to acknowledge His sovereignty in all areas of life. It urges us not to rely on our own understanding or human reasoning, but to put our faith in God's wisdom and guidance. The phrase "trust in the Lord with all your heart" emphasizes the importance of a deep, unwavering faith in God. It means that we should not only believe in God's existence, but also place our trust in His character, promises, and plans for our lives. The next line, "do not lean on your own understanding," reminds us that our own understanding is limited and fallible. We cannot always see the full picture, but God can. Therefore, we should not try to figure everything out on our own, but instead submit to God's will and wisdom. The final line, "he will make straight your paths," is a promise that God will guide us on the right path if we trust in Him and acknowledge Him in all our ways. This does not necessarily mean that life will be easy or without obstacles, but it does mean that we can have confidence that God is leading us in the right direction and that He will ultimately work all things together for our good. Overall, Proverbs 3:5-6 encourages us to trust in God wholeheartedly, to seek His guidance in all aspects of life, and to believe that He will lead us on the right path.

b. **Isaiah 41:10**: This verse is a message of comfort and assurance from God to His people. It is a reminder that even in times of difficulty, we can trust in God's presence, strength, and faithfulness. The first line, "Fear not, for I am with you," reminds us that we do not need to be afraid because God is always with us. His presence brings comfort, protection, and peace. The second line, "be not dismayed, for I am your God," emphasizes that God is our God, and we belong to Him. We do not need to be overwhelmed or discouraged because we are in His hands. The next three lines, "I will strengthen you, I will help you, I will uphold you with my righteous right hand," are a powerful promise from God. He promises to give us the strength we need to face our challenges, to help us when we are in trouble, and to uphold us with His righteous right hand, which symbolizes His power and authority. Overall, Isaiah 41:10 is a message of hope and encouragement that reminds us that we can trust in God's presence, strength, and faithfulness no matter what we are facing. It encourages us to turn to God in times of trouble and to rely on His promises to give us the help and support we need.

2. **Embracing God's Purpose for Each Season**

Understanding that God has a purpose for every season of life can help us grow in faith:

a. **Ecclesiastes 3:1-8**: There is a time and a season for everything under heaven. Each season has a unique purpose, and we should trust that God is working in our lives through each one.

b. **Romans 8:28**: God works all things together for good for those who love Him and are called according to His purpose.

3. **Nurturing Spiritual Growth Through Spiritual Disciplines**

To grow in faith, we must consistently engage in spiritual disciplines:

a. **2 Timothy 3:16-17**: Studying the Scriptures is essential for our growth and equipping us for every good work.

b. **1 Thessalonians 5:16-18**: Regular prayer, thanksgiving, and rejoicing help us maintain a close relationship with God.

4. Relying on the Holy Spirit for Guidance and Strength

The Holy Spirit plays a vital role in our spiritual growth throughout life's seasons:

a. **John 14:26**: Jesus promised that the Holy Spirit would teach us and remind us of everything He had taught us.

b. **Galatians 5:22-23**: The Holy Spirit produces spiritual fruit in our lives, such as love, joy, peace, and patience, which are essential for growth in every season.

5. Being Rooted in Christian Community

Our faith is strengthened and nurtured through our relationships with fellow believers:

a. **Hebrews 10:24-25**: We are encouraged to meet regularly with other believers to encourage one another and grow in faith.

b. **Colossians 3:16**: Believers are called to teach and admonish one another in wisdom, through worship and the sharing of Scripture.

Conclusion

Growing in faith through every season of life requires intentionality, reliance on God, and an understanding of His purpose for each stage. By trusting God in all circumstances, embracing His purpose for our lives, nurturing spiritual growth through spiritual disciplines, relying on the Holy Spirit, and being rooted in Christian community, we can cling to our faith regardless of the trials we face and experience growth in every season.

Chapter 10: Becoming a Spiritual Person and Maintaining Your Spirituality

10.1 Deepening Your Relationship with God

1. Abiding in Christ

To deepen your relationship with God, it's vital to abide in Jesus Christ:

a. **John 15:4-5**: Jesus teaches that we must abide in Him, and He will abide in us. Apart from Him, we can do nothing.

b. **Galatians 2:20**: Paul affirms that he has been crucified with Christ, and it is no longer he who lives, but Christ lives in him.

2. Prioritizing Prayer

Prayer is essential for maintaining and deepening our relationship with God:

a. **Philippians 4:6-7**: This passage is a reminder that we do not need to be anxious or worried about anything, but we can bring our concerns to God in prayer and find peace in His presence. The first line, "Do not be anxious about anything," encourages us to trust in God and not let our worries consume us. We can give our concerns to Him in prayer and trust that He will take care of us. The next line, "but in everything by prayer and supplication with thanksgiving let your requests be made known to God," reminds us to bring our requests to God in prayer, with thankfulness for all that He has done for us. We can ask God for help, guidance, and provision, knowing that He is always listening and ready to answer. The final line, "And the peace of God, which surpasses all understanding, will guard your hearts and your minds in Christ Jesus," promises us that God's peace, which is beyond our understanding, will protect us from anxiety and guard our hearts and minds. This peace comes from knowing that we are loved and cared for by God, and that He is in control of all things. Overall, Philippians 4:6-7 encourages us to turn to God in prayer and find peace in His presence. It reminds us that we do not need to be anxious or worried, but we can trust in God's love and care for us, and find rest in His peace.

b. **1 Thessalonians 5:17**: Paul instructs believers to "pray without ceasing."

3. Studying and Meditating on God's Word

A deep understanding of the Bible is crucial for spiritual growth:

a. **2 Timothy 2:15**: This verse is a call to believers to strive for excellence in their Christian walk, to be diligent in their study of God's word, and to live in a way that brings honor to God. The first line, "Do your best to present yourself to God as one approved," encourages us to live our lives in a way that pleases God. We should aim to be approved by God, not by others, and to live in a way that reflects His character and values. The next line, "a worker who has no need to be ashamed," reminds us that our lives should be characterized by hard work and diligence. We should be diligent in our study of God's word and in our efforts to live according to His will. If we are faithful in this, we will have no reason to be ashamed. The final line, "rightly handling the word of truth," emphasizes the importance of correctly understanding and applying God's word. We should study the Bible carefully, seeking to understand its meaning in context, and applying its teachings to our lives in a way that honors God. Overall, 2 Timothy 2:15 is a call to believers to live their lives in a way that pleases God, to be diligent in their study of His word, and to live in a way that reflects His character and values. By doing so, we can be approved by God and live a life that brings glory to Him.

b. **Joshua 1:8**: This verse is part of God's instruction to Joshua, who was appointed by God to lead the Israelites into the Promised Land after the death of Moses. The verse is a reminder of the importance of meditating on and obeying God's word. The first line, "This Book of the Law shall not depart from your mouth," emphasizes the importance of continually speaking God's word and making it a part of our lives. We should not only read the Bible, but also speak its truths and principles, so that they become a part of our daily conversations and interactions with others. The next line, "but you shall meditate on it day and night," reminds us of the importance of reflecting on and contemplating God's word. We should study the Bible carefully, seeking to understand its meaning in context and applying its teachings to our lives. The third line, "so that you may be careful to do according to all that is written in it," emphasizes the importance of obedience to God's word. It is not enough to simply read and study the Bible; we must also obey its teachings and apply them to our lives. The final line, "For then you will make your way prosperous, and then you will have good success," promises us that obedience to God's word will lead to prosperity and success. This does not necessarily mean material wealth or worldly success, but rather a life that is blessed and fruitful according to God's will. Overall, Joshua 1:8 is a reminder of the importance of meditating on and obeying God's word. It encourages us to make the Bible a central part of our lives, to reflect on its teachings, and to apply them to our lives in a way that honors God. By doing so, we can experience the blessings and prosperity that come from living a life that is aligned with God's will.

4. Cultivating the Fruit of the Spirit

As we grow in our relationship with God, the Holy Spirit produces spiritual fruit in our lives:

a. **Galatians 5:22-23**: The fruit of the Spirit includes love, joy, peace, patience, kindness, goodness, faithfulness, gentleness, and self-control.

b. **Ephesians 5:18-21**: Being filled with the Holy Spirit leads to a life of worship, gratitude, and submission to one another.

5. Participating in Christian Community

Fellowship with other believers is essential for deepening our relationship with God:

a. **Hebrews 10:24-25**: We are encouraged to gather together to inspire love, good works, and mutual encouragement.

b. **Acts 2:42-47**: The early church devoted themselves to fellowship, teaching, prayer, and sharing of possessions.

6. **Serving Others and Sharing the Gospel**

As we deepen our relationship with God, we are called to serve others and share the good news of Jesus:

a. **Matthew 28:19-20**: Jesus commissions His followers to make disciples of all nations, baptizing and teaching them.

b. **Galatians 6:9-10**: Paul encourages believers to do good to all, especially fellow believers, as they have the opportunity.

Conclusion

Becoming a spiritual person and maintaining your spirituality requires intentionality and discipline. Deepening your relationship with God involves abiding in Christ, prioritizing prayer, studying and meditating on God's Word, cultivating the fruit of the Spirit, participating in Christian community, and serving others and sharing the Gospel. By consistently engaging in these practices, believers can grow in their spirituality and enjoy a more profound relationship with God.

10.2 Developing a Consistent Prayer and Meditation Practice

1. **The Importance of Prayer**

Prayer is vital in our relationship with God, as it allows us to communicate with Him and seek His guidance and provision:

a. **Philippians 4:6-7**: We should present our requests to God with thanksgiving, and the peace of God will guard our hearts and minds.

b. **1 Thessalonians 5:16-18**: Paul exhorts believers to rejoice always, pray without ceasing, and give thanks in all circumstances.

2. **The Significance of Meditation**

Meditation on God's Word and His works helps us to grow in our understanding and appreciation of Him:

a. **Psalm 1:1-3**: The person who meditates on the law of the Lord day and night is like a tree planted by streams of water, bearing fruit in season.

b. **Psalm 119:15-16**: The psalmist declares their intention to meditate on God's precepts and fix their eyes on His ways.

3. Developing a Consistent Prayer Practice

Building a consistent prayer life involves intentional habits and routines:

a. **Mark 1:35**: Jesus often withdrew to solitary places to pray, demonstrating the importance of finding time and space for focused communication with God.

b. **Daniel 6:10**: Daniel maintained a consistent prayer practice, praying three times a day, even in the face of adversity.

4. Cultivating a Regular Meditation Routine

Consistent meditation on Scripture and God's works can help deepen our spirituality:

a. **Joshua 1:8**: Meditating on God's Word day and night leads to success in living according to His will.

b. **Psalm 63:6**: The psalmist meditates on God during the night watches, reflecting on His faithfulness.

5. Integrating Prayer and Meditation

Combining prayer and meditation can enrich our spiritual lives:

a. **Psalm 19:14**: The psalmist prays for the meditation of their heart and the words of their mouth to be acceptable to God.

b. **Colossians 4:2**: Paul encourages the Colossian church to be devoted to prayer while being watchful and thankful.

6. The Role of Accountability and Fellowship

Fellowship with other believers can help maintain consistency in our prayer and meditation practices:

a. **James 5:16**: Believers are encouraged to confess their sins to one another and pray for one another.

b. **Acts 1:14**: The early disciples gathered together in the upper room, devoting themselves to prayer in one accord.

Conclusion

Becoming a spiritual person and maintaining your spirituality requires developing a consistent prayer and meditation practice. This involves understanding the importance of prayer and meditation, creating intentional habits and routines, integrating both practices, and seeking accountability and fellowship with other believers. By dedicating time and effort to these practices, we can grow in our relationship with God and experience a deeper spiritual life.

10.3 Engaging in Regular Bible Study and Reflection

1. The Importance of Bible Study

Studying the Bible is crucial for spiritual growth, as it is God's primary means of revealing His character, will, and purposes to us:

a. **2 Timothy 3:16-17**: This passage emphasizes the importance and authority of Scripture in the life of a believer, and how it can equip us for every good work.

The first line, "All Scripture is breathed out by God," highlights the divine inspiration and authority of the Bible. It is not merely a human book, but it is the Word of God, given to us for our benefit and instruction.

The next line, "and profitable for teaching, for reproof, for correction, and for training in righteousness," explains the benefits of studying Scripture. It can teach us about God, correct our wrong thinking or behavior, and train us to live according to God's standards.

The final line, "that the man of God may be complete, equipped for every good work," emphasizes the practical application of Scripture. By studying and obeying God's word, we can be equipped for every good work, and become the kind of people God wants us to be.

Overall, 2 Timothy 3:16-17 is a powerful reminder of the importance and authority of Scripture in the life of a believer. It encourages us to study God's word diligently, seeking to understand its teachings and apply them to our lives. By doing so, we can be equipped to live in a way that honors God, and to do the good works that He has prepared for us.

b. **Hebrews 4:12**: This verse emphasizes the power and authority of God's word, and its ability to penetrate the depths of our hearts and reveal our true thoughts and intentions.

The first line, "For the word of God is living and active," emphasizes that the Bible is not a dead text, but a living, breathing expression of God's character and purposes. It has the power to transform our lives, not just intellectually, but also spiritually and emotionally.

The next line, "sharper than any two-edged sword," compares the power of God's word to that of a sharp sword, which can cut through even the toughest of materials. The Bible has the power to penetrate our hearts and reveal the deepest truths about ourselves.

The third line, "piercing to the division of soul and of spirit, of joints and of marrow," emphasizes that the power of God's word is not limited to the surface level of our lives, but can penetrate the very depths of our being. It can expose our innermost thoughts and desires, and reveal the true condition of our hearts.

The final line, "and discerning the thoughts and intentions of the heart," reminds us that the Bible has the power to reveal our true motives and intentions, even when we try to hide them. It can expose our hidden sins and idols, and show us the path to true repentance and healing.

Overall, Hebrews 4:12 is a powerful reminder of the authority and transformative power of God's word. It encourages us to study the Bible carefully, seeking to understand its teachings and applying them to our lives. By doing so, we can be transformed from the inside out, and live in a way that honors God and reflects His character.

2. Approaching Bible Study with the Right Attitude

We should approach Bible study with reverence, humility, and a teachable spirit:

a. **Psalm 119:18**: The psalmist prays for God to open their eyes to see the wonders in His Word.

b. **James 1:21**: We should humbly accept the Word that has been planted in us, which can save us.

3. The Practice of Regular Bible Study

Consistency in Bible study is essential for spiritual growth and maintaining a vibrant relationship with God:

a. **Acts 17:11**: This verse describes the response of the Jews in the city of Berea to the teachings of the apostle Paul. It emphasizes the importance of examining the Scriptures carefully to discern the truth and apply it to our lives.

The first line, "Now these Jews were more noble than those in Thessalonica," highlights the positive attitude of the Bereans towards the teachings of Paul. Unlike the Jews in Thessalonica, they were open and receptive to the message of the Gospel.

The next line, "they received the word with all eagerness," emphasizes the eagerness and enthusiasm of the Bereans in receiving the teachings of Paul. They were not merely passive listeners, but actively engaged in the study and application of God's word.

The third line, "examining the Scriptures daily to see if these things were so," emphasizes the importance of careful study and discernment of God's word. The Bereans did not simply accept Paul's teachings at face value, but carefully examined the Scriptures to ensure that what he said was in line with God's truth.

Overall, Acts 17:11 encourages us to be like the Bereans, who were open and receptive to God's word, and who carefully examined the Scriptures to discern the truth. It reminds us that we should not simply accept what others tell us, but should always seek to understand and apply God's word for ourselves. By doing so, we can deepen our faith and grow in our understanding of God's truth.

b. **Deuteronomy 6:6-7**: God's people are commanded to have His words in their hearts and to teach them diligently to their children, discussing them throughout daily life.

4. Employing Effective Bible Study Methods

Effective Bible study methods can help us understand and apply God's Word:

a. **Ezra 7:10**: Ezra prepared his heart to study the Law of the Lord, practice it, and teach it to others.

b. **2 Timothy 2:15**: Paul exhorts Timothy to rightly handle the Word of truth, implying the need for careful study and interpretation.

5. Reflecting on Scripture for Transformation

Meditating on God's Word allows it to impact our hearts, minds, and actions:

a. **Psalm 119:11**: The psalmist hides God's Word in their heart to avoid sinning against Him.

b. **Romans 12:2**: This verse is a call to believers to resist the influence of the world and instead allow God to transform their minds, so that they can discern His will and live according to His purposes.

The first line, "Do not be conformed to this world," warns us against allowing the values and priorities of the world to shape our thinking and behavior. We should not conform to the ways of the world, but instead seek to live according to God's standards.

The next line, "but be transformed by the renewal of your mind," reminds us that transformation is possible through the work of the Holy Spirit in our lives. We can be changed from the inside out as we allow God to renew our minds and transform our thinking.

The third line, "that by testing you may discern what is the will of God," emphasizes the importance of discerning God's will for our lives. This requires testing and discernment, which can only come through a transformed mind and a renewed perspective.

The final line, "what is good and acceptable and perfect," reminds us that God's will is good, acceptable, and perfect. It is not just a set of rules or regulations, but a way of life that is in line with God's character and purposes.

Overall, Romans 12:2 is a call to believers to resist the influence of the world and allow God to transform their minds. It encourages us to seek God's will and to live according to His purposes, which are good, acceptable, and perfect. By doing so, we can experience the fullness of life that comes from living in alignment with God's plan for us.

6. The Role of Community in Bible Study

Studying Scripture within a community of believers fosters encouragement, accountability, and growth:

a. **Colossians 3:16**: Believers are instructed to let the Word of Christ dwell in them richly, teaching and admonishing one another.

b. **Hebrews 10:24-25**: This passage encourages believers to support and encourage one another in their faith, and to prioritize meeting together regularly.

The first line, "And let us consider how to stir up one another to love and good works," reminds us that as believers, we should be actively seeking to encourage and support one another in our walk with God. We should be looking for ways to help one another grow in love and good works, rather than being focused solely on our own spiritual growth.

The next line, "not neglecting to meet together, as is the habit of some," emphasizes the importance of regular fellowship with other believers. While it is possible to have a personal relationship with God, we are also called to be part of a community of believers, where we can support and encourage one another in our faith.

The next line, "but encouraging one another," reminds us that we should be actively encouraging and building up our fellow believers. This can include speaking words of encouragement, offering support during difficult times, and holding one another accountable in our spiritual growth.

The final line, "and all the more as you see the Day drawing near," reminds us that as we approach the end times, it is even more important to prioritize our fellowship with other believers. We should be seeking to encourage and support one another as we face the challenges and trials of the last days.

Overall, Hebrews 10:24-25 is a reminder of the importance of fellowship with other believers and encouraging one another in our faith. It encourages us to be active in building up our fellow believers, and to prioritize meeting together regularly as we approach the end times.

Conclusion

Becoming a spiritual person and maintaining your spirituality involves engaging in regular Bible study and reflection. Recognizing the importance of Bible study, approaching it with the right attitude, practicing consistency, employing effective methods, reflecting on Scripture, and participating in community all contribute to our spiritual growth and enable us to deepen our relationship with God.

10.4 Prioritizing Worship and Spiritual Growth

1. The Importance of Worship

Worship is central to our relationship with God, as it acknowledges His worthiness, character, and lordship:

a. **Psalm 29:2**: The psalmist urges us to ascribe to the Lord the glory due His name and to worship Him in the splendor of His holiness.

b. **John 4:23-24**: Jesus teaches that true worshipers will worship the Father in spirit and truth, for God is seeking such people to worship Him.

2. Personal and Corporate Worship

Both personal and corporate worship are essential for spiritual growth and maintaining a vibrant relationship with God:

a. **Psalm 63:1-4**: The psalmist expresses a personal longing for God in worship, even in the wilderness.

b. **Hebrews 10:25**: Believers are encouraged not to neglect gathering together for worship and encouragement.

3. The Role of Worship in Spiritual Growth

Worship fosters spiritual growth by drawing us closer to God and transforming us into His likeness:

a. **2 Corinthians 3:18**: As we behold the glory of the Lord in worship, we are transformed into His image.

b. **Psalm 16:11**: In God's presence, we find fullness of joy and eternal pleasures, which fuel our spiritual growth.

4. Cultivating a Lifestyle of Worship

Worship is not limited to specific times or places but should permeate every aspect of our lives:

a. **Romans 12:1**: Paul encourages believers to offer their bodies as living sacrifices, holy and pleasing to God, which is our spiritual act of worship.

b. **Colossians 3:17**: We are to do everything in the name of the Lord Jesus, giving thanks to God the Father through Him, which includes all aspects of our lives.

5. Prioritizing Spiritual Growth

Intentional efforts to grow spiritually are necessary for maintaining a vibrant relationship with God:

a. **1 Peter 2:2**: Peter urges believers to crave the pure spiritual milk of God's Word so that they may grow up in their salvation.

b. **2 Peter 3:18**: Peter encourages believers to grow in the grace and knowledge of Jesus Christ, our Lord and Savior.

6. Engaging in Spiritual Practices

Engaging in spiritual practices, such as prayer, Bible study, meditation, and fellowship, helps foster spiritual growth:

a. **Acts 2:42**: Early believers devoted themselves to the apostles' teaching, fellowship, breaking of bread, and prayer.

b. **1 Timothy 4:7-8**: Paul exhorts Timothy to train himself in godliness, which holds promise for both the present life and the life to come.

Conclusion

Becoming a spiritual person and maintaining your spirituality requires prioritizing worship and spiritual growth. Embracing the importance of worship, engaging in both personal and corporate worship, cultivating a lifestyle of worship, and actively participating in spiritual practices are all essential elements in fostering spiritual growth and deepening our relationship with God.

10.5 Building Meaningful Connections with Fellow Believers

1. The Importance of Fellowship

Fellowship with other believers is an essential component of spiritual growth and maintaining our spirituality:

a. **Hebrews 10:24-25**: The writer of Hebrews emphasizes the importance of meeting together to encourage one another in love and good works.

b. **Acts 2:42-47**: The early church demonstrated the value of fellowship by devoting themselves to the apostles' teaching, breaking bread, prayer, and sharing their lives with one another.

2. **Building Meaningful Connections**

Meaningful connections with fellow believers involve mutual support, encouragement, and accountability:

a. **Ecclesiastes 4:9-12**: Solomon highlights the benefits of companionship, stating that two are better than one, as they can support and uplift each other in times of need.

b. **Galatians 6:2**: Paul instructs believers to bear one another's burdens, fulfilling the law of Christ.

3. **The Role of Authenticity and Vulnerability**

Authenticity and vulnerability are vital for building deep and meaningful connections with fellow believers:

a. **James 5:16**: James encourages believers to confess their sins to one another and pray for each other so that they may be healed.

b. **2 Corinthians 12:9-10**: Paul openly shares his weaknesses, demonstrating that vulnerability allows for God's power to be displayed in our lives.

4. **The Practice of Hospitality**

Hospitality plays a significant role in fostering meaningful connections among believers:

a. **Romans 12:13**: Paul exhorts believers to practice hospitality, which involves opening our homes and lives to one another.

b. **1 Peter 4:9**: Peter emphasizes the importance of showing hospitality to one another without grumbling.

5. **Serving and Supporting One Another**

Serving and supporting fellow believers help to strengthen relationships within the Christian community:

a. **Galatians 5:13**: Believers are called to serve one another in love.

b. **1 Thessalonians 5:11**: Paul encourages believers to build one another up, seeking each other's growth and wellbeing.

6. Cultivating Unity and Love

Unity and love are essential for building meaningful connections with fellow believers:

a. **John 13:34-35**: Jesus instructs His followers to love one another as He has loved them, stating that this will be a sign to the world that they are His disciples.

b. **Ephesians 4:1-6**: Paul urges believers to maintain the unity of the Spirit in the bond of peace, emphasizing that there is one body, one Spirit, one Lord, one faith, one baptism, and one God.

Conclusion

Becoming a spiritual person and maintaining spirituality involve building meaningful connections with fellow believers. By emphasizing the importance of fellowship, engaging in authentic and vulnerable relationships, practicing hospitality, serving and supporting one another, and cultivating unity and love, believers can strengthen their relationships with each other and grow in their faith.

10.6 Serving Others and Demonstrating God's Love

1. Jesus' Example of Servanthood

As Christians, we are called to follow Jesus' example of servanthood:

a. **John 13:12-17**: Jesus washed His disciples' feet, demonstrating humility and service. He instructed His followers to do the same for one another.

b. **Philippians 2:5-8**: Paul encourages believers to have the same mindset as Christ, who humbled Himself and became a servant for the sake of others.

2. The Importance of Serving Others

Serving others is an essential aspect of Christian spirituality:

a. **Matthew 20:26-28**: Jesus taught that true greatness is found in serving others, not in seeking positions of authority and power.

b. **Galatians 5:13-14**: Paul reminds believers that they are called to freedom, but they should use that freedom to serve one another in love.

3. Demonstrating God's Love Through Service

By serving others, we reflect God's love and character to the world:

a. **1 John 3:16-18**: John emphasizes that believers should demonstrate God's love through actions, not just words, by meeting the needs of others.

b. **Matthew 25:34-40**: Jesus commends those who serve others in need, stating that when we serve the least of these, we serve Him.

4. The Spiritual Gifts and Serving

God has given spiritual gifts to believers to be used in service to others:

a. **1 Corinthians 12:4-7**: Paul explains that there are different gifts, but all are given by the same Spirit for the common good of the body of Christ.

b. **1 Peter 4:10-11**: Peter encourages believers to use their spiritual gifts to serve others, as good stewards of God's grace.

5. Serving Within the Church Community

Believers are called to serve one another within the church community:

a. **Romans 12:3-8**: Paul highlights the importance of recognizing our unique gifts and using them to serve others in the body of Christ.

b. **Ephesians 4:11-13**: Paul describes the roles within the church, such as apostles, prophets, evangelists, pastors, and teachers, which are given to equip the saints for the work of ministry and build up the body of Christ.

6. Serving Beyond the Church Community

Christians are also called to serve those outside of the church community:

a. **Luke 10:25-37**: The parable of the Good Samaritan illustrates the importance of showing love and compassion to others, regardless of their background or circumstances.

b. **James 1:27**: James states that pure and undefiled religion involves caring for orphans and widows in their distress and keeping oneself unstained by the world.

Conclusion

Becoming a spiritual person and maintaining spirituality involves serving others and demonstrating God's love. By following Jesus' example of servanthood, recognizing the importance of service, reflecting God's love through our actions, utilizing our spiritual gifts, and serving both within and beyond the church community, we can grow in our faith and reveal the love of Christ to a world in need.

Chapter 11: How to Deal with Anxiety

11.1 Acknowledging Anxiety and Turning to God

1. **Recognizing Anxiety**

The Bible acknowledges the reality of anxiety and offers guidance for dealing with it:

a. **Proverbs 12:25**: The writer of Proverbs recognizes that anxiety weighs down the heart, acknowledging the negative impact it can have on our well-being.

b. **1 Peter 5:7**: Peter encourages believers to cast all their anxieties on God, acknowledging that we may experience anxiety in our lives.

2. **Turning to God in Times of Anxiety**

When we experience anxiety, we should turn to God and seek His help:

a. **Psalm 34:4-6**: The psalmist shares how he sought the Lord in times of fear, and the Lord delivered him from his fears, encouraging others to do the same.

b. **Isaiah 41:10**: God reassures His people not to be afraid, for He is with them, providing strength, help, and support in times of anxiety.

3. **Praying and Trusting in God's Presence**

Prayer is a powerful tool to help alleviate anxiety and trust in God's presence:

a. **Philippians 4:6-7**: Paul encourages believers not to be anxious about anything, but to present their requests to God through prayer and thanksgiving. In doing so, the peace of God will guard their hearts and minds in Christ Jesus.

b. **Matthew 6:25-34**: Jesus teaches that we should not worry about our daily needs, for God knows and provides for them. Instead, we should seek God's kingdom and righteousness, trusting in His provision.

4. **Meditating on God's Word**

Focusing on God's Word can help alleviate anxiety and provide peace:

a. **Psalm 119:165**: The psalmist declares that those who love God's law have great peace and will not be easily shaken by anxiety.

b. **Joshua 1:8**: God instructs Joshua to meditate on His Word day and night, as this will lead to success and help him remain strong and courageous in the face of challenges.

5. **Finding Support from Fellow Believers**

We can find support and encouragement from fellow believers in times of anxiety:

a. **Galatians 6:2**: Paul urges believers to bear one another's burdens, fulfilling the law of Christ, which includes providing support in times of anxiety.

b. **1 Thessalonians 5:11**: Paul encourages believers to build each other up and provide support in times of need.

Conclusion

Dealing with anxiety from a biblical, comprehensive, and conservative Christian perspective involves acknowledging anxiety, turning to God for help, praying and trusting in God's presence, meditating on His Word, and finding support from fellow believers. By seeking God's guidance and relying on His strength, we can find peace and hope amidst anxiety.

11.2 Implementing Spiritual Practices for Anxiety Relief

1. Practicing Mindfulness and Meditation

Mindfulness and meditation can help us focus on God's presence and promises, alleviating anxiety:

a. **Psalm 46:10**: The psalmist encourages us to be still and know that God is in control, reminding us to focus on God's sovereignty in the midst of our anxiety.

b. **Psalm 1:1-3**: The psalmist describes the blessings that come from meditating on God's Word, including stability and fruitfulness in our lives, which can provide a sense of peace amidst anxiety.

2. Engaging in Prayer

Prayer is a powerful way to connect with God and find peace in times of anxiety:

a. **Philippians 4:6-7**: This passage is a reminder to believers that they should not be anxious or worried about anything, but rather bring their concerns to God in prayer and experience His peace.

The first line, "Do not be anxious about anything," encourages believers to trust in God and not to worry. We can give our worries and concerns to God in prayer, trusting that He will take care of us.

The next line, "but in everything by prayer and supplication with thanksgiving let your requests be made known to God," encourages believers to bring their requests to God in prayer. We can ask God for help, guidance, and provision, knowing that He is always listening and ready to answer. The act of giving thanks in prayer also helps to shift our focus from our problems to God's faithfulness.

The final line, "And the peace of God, which surpasses all understanding, will guard your hearts and your minds in Christ Jesus," promises believers that God's peace, which is beyond human understanding, will guard their hearts and minds. This peace comes from knowing that we are loved and cared for by God, and that He is in control of all things.

Overall, Philippians 4:6-7 encourages believers to turn to God in prayer and find peace in His presence. It reminds us that we do not need to be anxious or worried, but we can trust in God's love and care for us and find rest in His peace.

b. **James 5:13**: James encourages believers to pray when they are in trouble, recognizing that God hears and responds to our prayers.

3. Memorizing and Reciting Scripture

Committing Scripture to memory and reciting it during anxious moments can bring comfort and peace:

a. **Deuteronomy 6:6-9**: This passage emphasizes the importance of taking God's commands to heart and passing them on to future generations in both word and deed.

The first line, "And these words that I command you today shall be on your heart," emphasizes the importance of internalizing God's commands and making them a part of our lives. We should not simply memorize or recite God's commands, but we should truly believe them and live them out in our daily lives.

The next lines, "You shall teach them diligently to your children, and shall talk of them when you sit in your house, and when you walk by the way, and when you lie down, and when you rise," emphasize the importance of passing on God's commands to future generations. We should not only live out God's commands ourselves, but also actively teach them to our children and others around us. This can be done in a variety of settings, including at home, on the go, and before going to bed and after waking up.

The following lines, "You shall bind them as a sign on your hand, and they shall be as frontlets between your eyes. You shall write them on the doorposts of your house and on your gates," encourage believers to display God's commands visibly in their homes and on their bodies. This can serve as a constant reminder to ourselves and others of the importance of living out God's commands.

Overall, Deuteronomy 6:6-9 emphasizes the importance of internalizing God's commands, passing them on to future generations, and displaying them visibly in our homes and on our bodies. By doing so, we can ensure that God's commands remain central in our lives and that they continue to be passed down to future generations.

b. **Psalm 119:11**: This verse highlights the importance of memorizing and meditating on God's word as a way of guarding our hearts against sin.

The first line, "I have stored up your word in my heart," emphasizes the importance of memorizing and internalizing God's word. When we commit God's word to memory and meditate on it regularly, it becomes a part of us, shaping our thoughts and actions.

The next line, "that I might not sin against you," highlights the practical benefits of storing God's word in our hearts. By meditating on God's word, we can gain wisdom and insight into how to live according to His will. This can help us to avoid sin and live in a way that honors God.

Overall, Psalm 119:11 encourages us to store God's word in our hearts, meditating on it regularly and allowing it to shape our thoughts and actions. By doing so, we can gain wisdom and insight into how to live according to God's will and avoid sin.

4. **Worship and Praise**

Worshipping God through praise and music can help refocus our minds on God's goodness and alleviate anxiety:

a. **Colossians 3:16**: Paul instructs believers to let the message of Christ dwell among them and to teach and admonish one another through worship, helping to create a supportive environment for anxiety relief.

b. **Psalm 95:1-3**: The psalmist invites believers to come before God with thanksgiving and praise, acknowledging His greatness and sovereignty over all things.

5. **Seeking Community and Support**

Finding solace in a community of believers can provide encouragement and support during times of anxiety:

a. **Hebrews 10:24-25**: Believers are encouraged to gather together, spur one another on, and encourage each other, which can provide support during anxious times.

b. **Ecclesiastes 4:9-12**: The author emphasizes the importance of companionship and support, noting that two are better than one, as they can help each other through difficult circumstances, including anxiety.

Conclusion

Dealing with anxiety from a biblical, comprehensive, and conservative Christian perspective involves implementing spiritual practices for anxiety relief, such as mindfulness, meditation, prayer, Scripture memorization, worship, and seeking community support. By engaging in these practices, we can refocus our minds on God's presence, promises, and power, helping us find peace and hope in the midst of anxiety.

11.3 Trusting in God's Control and Sovereignty

1. Recognizing God's Sovereignty

Trusting in God's control and sovereignty is essential for overcoming anxiety. The Bible is filled with reminders of God's ultimate authority over all creation:

a. **Psalm 103:19**: The psalmist declares that God's throne is in heaven, and His sovereignty rules over all, emphasizing God's ultimate control over everything.

b. **Isaiah 46:9-10**: The Lord asserts His uniqueness and power, declaring that He knows the end from the beginning and that His purpose will stand.

2. Trusting in God's Goodness and Love

Believing in God's goodness and love can provide comfort and reassurance during times of anxiety:

a. **Romans 8:28**: This verse offers comfort and reassurance to believers that God is in control and that everything that happens is part of His plan.

The first part of the verse, "And we know that for those who love God all things work together for good," emphasizes that God is working in all things, even difficult or challenging situations, to bring about good. This doesn't necessarily mean that everything that happens is good in and of itself, but rather that God can use it for good and to accomplish His purposes.

The second part of the verse, "for those who are called according to his purpose," emphasizes that this promise is for those who are following God's call and living according to His purposes. This promise is not for everyone, but for those who are seeking to live in obedience to God and to fulfill His plan for their lives.

Overall, Romans 8:28 is a reminder that God is in control, and that He can bring good out of even the most difficult situations. It encourages believers to trust in God's plan and to continue to follow His call, even when things seem uncertain or difficult.

b. **Psalm 145:8-9**: The psalmist praises God's goodness and mercy, proclaiming that the Lord is gracious, compassionate, and good to all.

3. **Leaning on God's Wisdom**

Understanding that God's wisdom surpasses our own can help us trust Him during anxious times:

a. **Proverbs 3:5-6**: Solomon advises us to trust in the Lord with all our hearts and not to rely on our own understanding, but to acknowledge God in all our ways, and He will direct our paths.

b. **Isaiah 55:8-9**: The Lord states that His thoughts and ways are higher than our own, emphasizing the need to trust in His wisdom during times of anxiety.

4. **Resting in God's Promises**

Relying on God's promises can provide strength and comfort when we face anxiety:

a. **Matthew 6:25-34**: In this passage, Jesus tells His listeners not to worry about their lives, including what they will eat, drink, or wear. He reminds them that God cares for them and will provide for their needs, just as He does for the birds of the air and the flowers of the field.

Jesus also emphasizes the futility of worry, pointing out that it cannot add anything to our lives. He encourages His listeners to seek first God's kingdom and righteousness, trusting that all their needs will be provided for.

The passage ends with the reassurance that God knows our needs and will provide for us, as long as we seek Him first and trust in His care.

Overall, Matthew 6:25-34 is a powerful reminder of the importance of trusting in God and not worrying about our material needs. It encourages us to seek first God's kingdom and righteousness, trusting that all our needs will be met according to His plan and purpose.

b. **Philippians 4:19**: Paul assures believers that God will supply all their needs according to His riches in Christ Jesus, emphasizing God's provision and care.

Conclusion

Dealing with anxiety from a biblical, comprehensive, and conservative Christian perspective involves trusting in God's control and sovereignty. By recognizing God's authority, believing in His goodness and love, leaning on His wisdom, and resting in His promises, we can find peace and hope during times of anxiety. These foundational beliefs can help us navigate life's challenges with faith and trust in God's unchanging character and His perfect plan for our lives.

11.4 Developing a Balanced and God-Centered Lifestyle

1. **Prioritizing Time with God**

A balanced and God-centered lifestyle begins with prioritizing time with God through prayer, Bible study, and worship:

a. **Psalm 1:1-3**: The psalmist describes the person who delights in the law of the Lord and meditates on it day and night as being like a tree planted by streams of water, yielding fruit in its season.

b. **Mark 1:35**: Jesus sets an example for us by prioritizing time alone with God in prayer, even amidst His busy ministry.

2. **Practicing Self-Care**

Taking care of our physical, emotional, and mental well-being is important in maintaining a balanced lifestyle:

a. **1 Corinthians 6:19-20**: Paul reminds believers that their bodies are temples of the Holy Spirit and encourages them to honor God with their bodies.

b. **Mark 6:31**: Jesus invites His disciples to come away to a quiet place and rest, acknowledging the need for rest and self-care.

3. **Fostering Healthy Relationships**

Cultivating strong connections with family, friends, and fellow believers is essential for a balanced and God-centered lifestyle:

a. **Proverbs 27:17**: Solomon emphasizes the importance of friendships that sharpen and encourage one another in their walk with God.

b. **Hebrews 10:24-25**: Believers are encouraged to not neglect meeting together, but to spur one another on toward love and good deeds.

4. **Serving Others**

A balanced and God-centered lifestyle involves serving others and sharing God's love:

a. **Galatians 5:13**: Paul instructs believers to serve one another humbly in love, reflecting the character of Christ.

b. **Matthew 25:40**: Jesus emphasizes the importance of serving others, stating that whatever we do for the least of His brothers and sisters, we do for Him.

5. Setting Priorities and Boundaries

Living a balanced lifestyle requires setting priorities and boundaries to prevent excessive busyness and stress:

a. **Matthew 6:33**: Jesus instructs His followers to seek first the kingdom of God and His righteousness, emphasizing the need to prioritize God's will in our lives.

b. **Ephesians 5:15-16**: Paul encourages believers to be wise in their use of time, making the most of every opportunity.

Conclusion

Dealing with anxiety from a biblical, comprehensive, and conservative Christian perspective involves developing a balanced and God-centered lifestyle. Prioritizing time with God, practicing self-care, fostering healthy relationships, serving others, and setting priorities and boundaries can help create a stable foundation for managing anxiety. As we strive for balance and prioritize our relationship with God, we can experience His peace and presence in our lives, even in the midst of challenges and uncertainties.

11.5 Seeking Professional Help and Support When Needed

1. Recognizing the Need for Help

The Bible encourages believers to seek help and support when facing struggles, including anxiety:

a. **Galatians 6:2**: Paul instructs Christians to bear one another's burdens, indicating that it is appropriate to seek assistance from others when facing difficulties.

b. **Proverbs 11:14**: Solomon emphasizes the importance of wise counsel, suggesting that seeking guidance from others can provide direction and support.

2. Utilizing God-Given Resources

God provides resources, including trained professionals, to help us navigate life's challenges:

a. **1 Corinthians 12:4-6**: Paul explains that there are various gifts and services given by the Holy Spirit, which can include professional skills like counseling or therapy.

b. **Romans 12:6-8**: Paul lists various gifts given to believers, including teaching and encouragement, which can be applicable to professional helpers who offer support and guidance.

3. Integrating Faith with Professional Help

Seeking professional help does not negate the importance of faith; rather, it can complement our spiritual growth and healing:

a. **2 Corinthians 1:3-4**: Paul describes God as the "Father of compassion and the God of all comfort," who comforts us in our troubles so that we can comfort others. Seeking professional help can be a way to receive and extend God's comfort to others in need.

b. **James 1:5**: James encourages believers to ask God for wisdom when facing trials, which can include seeking counsel from professionals equipped with knowledge and expertise.

4. Finding Support in Community

In addition to professional help, it is important to maintain connections with fellow believers and share our struggles:

a. **Ecclesiastes 4:9-10**: Solomon highlights the value of companionship, noting that when one person falls, the other can provide help and support.

b. **Hebrews 3:13**: The author of Hebrews encourages believers to encourage and support one another daily, demonstrating the significance of mutual care within the faith community.

Conclusion

Dealing with anxiety from a biblical, comprehensive, and conservative Christian perspective can involve seeking professional help and support when needed. The Bible encourages believers to seek assistance, utilize God-given resources, integrate faith with professional help, and find support in community. By recognizing the value of professional support and maintaining connections with fellow believers, Christians can navigate anxiety and grow stronger in their faith.

11.6 Encouraging Others and Sharing Your Testimony

Anxiety is a common mental health issue that affects many individuals, regardless of their background, gender, or age. The Bible acknowledges the reality of anxiety and provides guidance on how to manage it. As Christians, we can find comfort and peace in God's Word and His promises. We are called to trust in God and His sovereignty, seek His wisdom and guidance, and support and encourage one another.

One way to deal with anxiety is by encouraging others and sharing our testimonies. When we share our experiences and how God has helped us overcome anxiety, we can provide hope and encouragement to those who are struggling with similar issues. The Bible encourages us to bear one another's burdens and to be there for each other in times of need. By sharing our struggles and how God has helped us, we can build each other up and support one another.

The book of James reminds us to "consider it pure joy, my brothers and sisters, whenever you face trials of many kinds, because you know that the testing of your faith produces perseverance" (James 1:2-3). While anxiety may feel overwhelming and daunting, we can trust that God is using it to strengthen our faith and character. Through our struggles, we can become more resilient and persevere through difficult times.

As Christians, we are called to be the light of the world and to share the love of Christ with others. When we encourage and support those who are struggling with anxiety, we are fulfilling this calling. We can share our testimonies and how God has helped us overcome anxiety through prayer, reading the Bible, seeking counseling, or relying on the support of our church community.

Additionally, we can provide practical support by offering to pray with and for those who are struggling, providing resources such as books or devotionals, or simply being a listening ear. The Bible reminds us that we should "encourage one another and build each other up" (1 Thessalonians 5:11). By encouraging others, we can help them feel loved and valued and remind them that they are not alone in their struggles.

Sharing our testimonies can also help us gain a better understanding of God's faithfulness and provision. When we look back on how God has helped us overcome anxiety in the past, we can find hope and reassurance for the future. The psalmist writes, "I sought the Lord, and he answered me; he delivered me from all my fears" (Psalm 34:4). When we turn to God in prayer and seek His help, we can trust that He will answer us and provide us with the peace and comfort we need.

In addition to sharing our testimonies, there are other biblical practices that can help us deal with anxiety. For example, prayer and meditation on God's Word can help us focus on His promises and find peace in His presence. Philippians 4:6-7 says, "Do not be anxious about anything, but in every situation, by prayer and petition, with thanksgiving, present your requests to God. And the peace of God, which transcends all understanding, will guard your hearts and your minds in Christ Jesus."

Regularly attending church and connecting with other believers can also help us manage anxiety. Being part of a community that supports and encourages us can provide us with a sense of belonging and purpose. Additionally, we can seek out professional help if needed, such as seeing a therapist or counselor. While anxiety is a normal part of life, it can become debilitating if left untreated. Seeking professional help is a sign of strength and a way to prioritize our mental health.

By sharing our testimonies and experiences of overcoming anxiety with others, we can offer hope and encouragement to those who may be struggling with the same challenges. It is important to remember that anxiety is a common struggle, but with God's help, we can overcome it.

It is also essential to seek professional help and support when needed. Seeking guidance from a Christian counselor or therapist can provide additional tools and resources for managing anxiety in a healthy and effective way. It is not a sign of weakness to ask for help, but rather a step towards healing and growth.

Finally, cultivating a lifestyle centered on God and His Word can help us manage anxiety and promote overall well-being. Regular prayer, meditation, and Bible study can provide a sense of peace and security, as we are reminded of God's love, faithfulness, and sovereignty over all circumstances.

In summary, dealing with anxiety as a Christian involves acknowledging and turning to God, implementing spiritual practices, seeking professional help and support, encouraging others, and cultivating a God-centered lifestyle. Through these steps, we can find hope, healing, and freedom from anxiety, and grow closer to God in the process.

BIBLIOGRAPHY

Trusting God: Even When Life Hurts by Jerry Bridges

Hope for the Troubled Heart: Finding God in the Midst of Pain by Billy Graham

Finding God in the Hard Times: Choosing to Trust and Hope When You Can't See the Way by Matt and Beth Redman

Anxious for Nothing: Finding Calm in a Chaotic World by Max Lucado

God's Promises for Your Every Need by Jack Countryman

The Power of Prayer and Fasting: 21 Days That Can Change Your Life by Marilyn Hickey

God Is With You Every Day by Max Lucado

Peace with God: The Secret of Happiness by Billy Graham

Spiritual Disciplines Handbook: Practices That Transform Us by Adele Ahlberg Calhoun

Running Scared: Fear, Worry, and the God of Rest by Edward T. Welch

Hope When You're Hurting: Answers to Four Questions Hurting People Ask by Larry Crabb

The Anxiety Cure: You Can Find Emotional Tranquility and Wholeness by Dr. Archibald D. Hart

Unstuck: Your Life. God's Design. Real Change. by Arnie Cole and Michael Ross

The Calm My Anxious Heart: A Woman's Guide to Finding Contentment by Linda Dillow

A Grace Disguised: How the Soul Grows through Loss by Jerry Sittser

The Sacred Romance: Drawing Closer to the Heart of God by Brent Curtis and John Eldredge

Victory Over the Darkness: Realizing the Power of Your Identity in Christ by Neil T. Anderson

God's Wisdom for Navigating Life: A Year of Daily Devotions in the Book of Proverbs by Timothy Keller

A Grief Observed by C.S. Lewis

www.ingramcontent.com/pod-product-compliance
Lightning Source LLC
Chambersburg PA
CBHW060155050426
42446CB00013B/2844